Brother Dog

Southern Tales & Hollywood Adventures

Harry Thomason

Harry Thomason

T0307891

Parkhurst Brothers Publishers
MARION, MICHIGAN

www.parkhurstbrothers.com

Parkhurst Brothers Publishers is located at 110 West Main Street, Marion, Michigan 49665. Copies of this and other Parkhurst Brothers Publishers titles are available to churches, organizations and corporations for purchase in quantity by contacting Special Sales Department at our home office location, listed on our web site. Manuscript submission guidelines for this publishing company are available at our web site. All photographs courtesy of the Thomason family.

Printed in the United States of America

First Hardback Edition, 2019

2019 2020 2021 2022   10 9 8 7 6 5 4 3 2 1

Cataloging Data:
1. Title–Brother Dog: Southern Tales and Hollywood Adventures.
2. Author: Harry Thomason
3. Subject: memoir-southern regional, entrepreneurship
c. pm. Original trade paperback, 2019
life stories by a noted film director

Hardback ISBN: 978-1-62491-138-5
E-Book ISBN: 971-1-62491-139-2

Dustjacket and page design by: Linda D. Parkhurst, Ph.D.
Acquired for Parkhurst Brothers and edited by: Ted Parkhurst
Proofread by: Bill and Barbara Paddack

102019

Dedication

For LBT
Loving you has been the greatest adventure of all.

Contents

A Note to the Reader

A FRIEND ONCE TOLD ME THAT HE ENJOYED READING MEMOIRS and biographies because he was strangely comforted to know that others who appeared outwardly successful had faced uncommon hurdles, seemingly insurmountable obstacles, seasons of crippling grief, and times of deep discouragement. My friend will find pitfalls, pratfalls, and obstacles aplenty in these stories.

I am blessed with enough aunts, uncles, cousins, and others—as well as my nuclear family—to fill a military barracks. From that family, I have learned to be compassionate, usually dutiful, and always observant. As an adult working in the business of storytelling, I've seen the power of observation, truthful reportage (even if in a drama), and reflection. These stories are the principal reflections of an old man who has found magic—and occasional profit—in telling tales that audiences bought tickets or tuned in to follow.

What won't be found in these stories are political opinions, partisan glorifications, or diatribes. This is not a book telling all I know about old friends, whether they be politicians, Hollywood actors, or musicians. Yes, you will find a few stories that touch on the interlacing of our lives with the Clintons (I have known Bill since his graduate school days). But, at its core, this is the story of a life—my life. If I ever decide to tell all I know about prominent friends, it will come in another book (one not actively in my life-plan today). Maybe I will include friends here in a small story or two, but that's not the focus of this volume. In the pages that follow, you will read about my small-town childhood antics, my little brother, Danny, and our brother, a dog named Ted. You will follow me through high school and college antics—some well-conceived, but most from the "lucky to survive" category. And you will hear about the dreams, struggles, and coincidences that have led me from the joys of coaching high school football to the frustrations and rewards of years producing and directing films and TV programs—both series and movies.

Fate has occasionally thrown me into the path of people whose names were household words, and I have reported those incidents where I thought the moment rose to the level of general interest, insight, or entertainment. Stories—and memory—are subjective, anyone who has been in the storytelling business as long as I have has learned that lesson (probably painfully) and has re-learned it more times than he would like to admit.

Here, you will discover stories of my gratitude for a banker named Randy, an ad man named Jim, a working man who put his buddies above himself, a lawyer who stooped to protect me from myself during my early days in the film business, and a woman I have been so incredibly fortunate to call my wife. My editor tells me you will enjoy the read. All I can say is thanks for sharing the journey.

Harry Thomason
Encino, California
June, 2019

Introduction
Linda Bloodworth Thomason

THESE STORIES ARE IMBUED WITH A BASIC HUMANITY and way of life seldom seen anymore. As the person who knows him best, I can assure you that Harry is the kindest and most reliable human being I've ever known. I believe I can trace the origin of Harry's good heart and steady character to the small, Arkansas town where he grew up. His parents owned a little store, where it was said they gave away more groceries than they sold. His mother used to joke that "The whole town raised Harry." You could check him out like a library book, take him fishing, or if you were the mail or milkman, you could even take him on your rounds. He was completely free-range, part of a posse of six year olds racing through the Arkansas woods, with Harry atop his favorite horse, Old Bird and his beloved dog, Ted, running alongside. As these stories suggest, his only boundary was his own imagination.

His daughter Stacy says, "Dad's the guy who always has his arm around the most left-out person in the room."

As his friend, President Bill Clinton says, "Harry not only shows up, but also stays for the dark night."

And then there's his legendary optimism. Actor Billy Bob

Thornton—who named his son after Harry—does a hilarious, spot-on imitation of him as the leader of the ill-fated Donner party delivering an electrifying, motivational speech to his fellow travelers.

I have always suspected the reason Harry is so comfortable in his own skin is because he traverses the world as though it's his little hometown writ large. He's just as copacetic hanging out in a black church with his family's maid, May Ethel (both of them spellbound by the music of a teenage B.B. King) as he would someday be while introducing British Prime Minister Tony Blair to Chuck Berry—Blair's childhood idol. He is just as at ease sitting on the porch, chatting with his fifty-year-old special needs cousin, Mervyn—"Mama, come outside! Ha-reee's here!"—as he would one day be, when discussing football over drinks with Sir Laurence Olivier.

Even the overly-ambitious fights he had with a much older and larger town bully, no doubt helped prepare him for future bouts of having to wrestle *Evening Shade* star Burt Reynolds to the ground (usually, for threating to beat up the writers). As one of them fondly recalls, "I'll never forget Harry's sweet, soft-spoken drawl saying, 'I'm not going to hurt you Burt, I'm just gonna hold you for awhile.'"

As I finish these warm and colorful pages, I feel fortunate to have shared my life with the man who wrote them. And lived them. And I am frankly awed by the beautiful, audacious women who made him possible. From his wise and enterprising mother to all of his aunts—especially the basketball-playing ones who often piled into Harry's room on game nights when it was too late to make it home. They are the ladies who gave him a lasting tutorial in rowdy, Southern feminism—alternately dazzling, molding and challenging him to be a better boy—and consequently, an even better man. Harry is the sort who loves, respects, and reveres women—especially the *Designing* kind.

I never wanted to be married. But luckily, Harry, who's a pilot, rented a small plane one day and flew it to my hometown in Missouri, where he called me and said, "Okay, your childhood bedroom is blue and I'm standing in it. I've just taken your parents to dinner and given them the horrific news that I've fallen in love with their daughter and am planning to ask her to marry me, as soon as I get back to California. They're shaken but seem to be thinking about it. I hope you're not gonna make me look bad." I didn't. That was the best decision I've ever made. In the end, I followed my father's life-long edict: Never marry a man unless he loves you as much as I love your mother."

Sadly, my dad did not live to see our wedding. On the last day of his life, he called me into his hospital room. As a former prosecutor all too familiar with poor male behavior, he had been less than enthusiastic about most of the young men I dated. He wanted me to know that he was at peace now. Invoking my childhood nickname, Daddy said, "Nawson, you were always bringing home boys ... You finally brought home a man." Then, squeezing my hand, he bestowed his highest and final accolade, "Harry's a peach." I smiled. Indeed.

The Killer Just Miles Away

TEXARKANA, TEXAS, 1946. On a chilly February night, Jimmy and Mary Jeanne were talking in Jimmy's car. It was a lonely road and a dark night. They never saw the man coming. Suddenly, the door was jerked open and the intruder, a burlap sack over his head, two slits for his eyes, was screaming, "Get out of the car, now!"

They went out into the black night. The intruder beat Jimmy with his handgun. What sounded like gunshots to Mary Jeanne was really the sound of Jimmy's skull being cracked by the pistol handle. The man then assaulted Mary Jeanne but fled as, without warning, a car approached.

Mary Jeanne and Jimmy were the lucky ones. They lived that February night. Most of the unnamed intruder's other victims were not going to be so fortunate.

Ninety-five miles away, I woke up in the early morning and stumbled into the kitchen to the smell of my mother's bacon, and preparing for another day in the first grade. My dad slurped his coffee, unfolded the newspaper, and read. My mom hummed as she stirred a pan of oatmeal for me. Something was different. They seemed distracted listening to KRLD, the radio station in El Dorado, a much larger, nearby town. Soon, I heard the news reporting last night's attack on the young couple.

In the early Twenty-First Century, we have become inured to random violent acts but in 1946 such an attack was unnerving. Nervously, I asked a few questions and was reassured by Mom such a thing "... will probably not happen again, besides, it was almost a hundred miles away! Don't worry."

At recess, my neighbor and good friend, Charlie, a third-grader, said his parents had been listening to their radio during breakfast, too. He asked if it scared me. Jauntily, I replied, "No, it's far away. It was all the way in Texas."

"No," Charlie says, "my dad says half of the town is in Arkansas." Okay, maybe I was actually a little nervous.

Over the next few weeks, the incident entirely slipped from my mind.

It was soon to return.

I came in from the yard where Charlie, a great storyteller, had just finished telling my friends about an imaginary trip to the moon. My mom stood motionless by the kitchen radio holding my two-year-old baby brother, Danny, in her arms. I listened, as the booming voice on CBS Radio recounted the grisly details of last night's double murder in Texarkana, Texas. Polly Ann Moore and Richard Griffin had been shot in the back of the head on a lonely road. Mom turned, saw me, and quickly reached to turn the radio off. At supper, when I asked about it, she told me not to fret. The murder was far away and in Texas.

I did fret. I couldn't fall asleep while hearing the muffled radio through my door. The announcer described an atmosphere of anxiety. People were nervous for miles around Texarkana because of reports that a killer was prowling the area. A term hadn't been invented for this type of crime yet, but it was about to be.

A media circus descended upon Texarkana. Reporters, mostly hardened men wearing fedoras and carrying wooden pencils and small notebooks in which they endlessly scratched, were shouting questions. A few carried microphones and fifty-pound audio recorders. TV was still five to ten years away in most markets.

Charlie said, "My dad hopes the killer comes here. Dad says he'd give that bad guy both barrels of his twelve-gauge shotgun." It was okay with me if he didn't come to Hampton, especially next door to Charlie's house.

Again, the scariness went away in a few weeks. Just as I was beginning to sleep soundly, it happened again.

Betty Jo Booker and Paul Martin were shot dead. She was attacked before she was murdered. It was all over the newspapers, magazines and radio stations. Now Satan had a name: The Phantom Killer. This was big. *Time, Newsweek,* and *Look* magazine teams arrived in Texarkana to report on it. Charlie and I sat on the doorstep as darkness slowly covered the town. "Dad thinks it might be a policeman. I want to go to Texarkana," Charlie says.

"Why would you want to do that?" I asked.

Mom interrupted before he could answer, "Okay guys, time to get inside, it's dark. Charlie, I'll watch until you get through the door." Funny, she never made us come in because it was dark *before* and she had never watched Charlie as he crossed our yard into his house. She had her arm around me as she waved Charlie through his back door.

That night the radio said that people in almost every home in Texarkana were sleeping with guns near their beds. As Mom was tucking me into bed, I could hear the NBC radio network reporting that even as far away as Oklahoma City terrified people were arming themselves.

"Mom, how far is Oklahoma City from Texarkana?"

"About three hundred miles."

"Gosh, we're just ninety-something miles away!"

"It's okay. Go to sleep, honey. I love you." She kissed me, turned out the lamp, and walked out. I lay in the darkness. Scared.

～

Children in my town no longer stayed out after dark. Cars on the street were rare after nine o'clock at night. Teenagers stopped dating—at least in cars—after dark. The movie theaters in nearby El Dorado canceled evening showings of Burt Lancaster and Ava Gardner in *The Killers* and sat empty after dark.

Charlie kept thinking of ways we could trap the guy if we could just get his dad to take us to Texarkana. Later, I heard the sound of the radio wafting through my door as my parents listened to the late-night edition of CBS news. "I'm Walter Cronkite and this is *CBS Radio News*. Tonight, famed Texas Ranger Manuel

'Lone Wolf' Gonzaullas arrived in Texarkana, the town straddling the border of Texas and Arkansas. He vowed to use every resource to stop the horrible killing spree in this small town ..." As I lay in the dark listening to the sound of distant traffic, I drifted off to sleep earlier than usual. The Rangers were here!

For a month, it was very quiet, people even began staying out late again, and the movie business in Texarkana and elsewhere went back to normal. The Rangers might not have caught anyone, but their vigilance was keeping the beast from striking again.

That illusion ended abruptly on May third at an isolated farmhouse located three miles northeast of Texarkana, when Virgil Starks was shot to death by The Phantom Killer. His wife heard the shots and ran to the phone only to meet two gunshots to the face. As the killer slipped into the woods, Mrs. Starks managed to run out the front door to a neighbor's house. She survived but could not provide a description of the killer.

There was one other thing, these victims were on the Arkansas side of the border. "Mom, the person that hurts people is now in Arkansas?"

"It's okay, he's still very far away." A little comfort but not entirely convincing. That night, I noticed my dad carrying something down the hallway into their room. I watched as he carefully placed his deer-rifle under his side of the bed. He didn't know I saw him, but it induced a terror-filled night. I loaded my Roy Rogers six-shooter with caps and placed it under my pillow. *Can't be too careful.*

I wish this story had a great ending where the Ranger caught the killer. But sometimes life doesn't tidy itself up before it moves on. Weeks then months passed with no more killings. Finally, the charismatic Ranger moved himself and his cohorts out of town—quietly so the killer would not know they were gone. And that was it, no more killings. The circus left town and the murders faded from the news. America was left with a new phrase in its vocabulary, *serial killer.*

In 1946, television barely existed. You could only read newspapers, listen to the radio, and let your imagination fill in the picture. No camera can ever produce an image more terrifying than your imagination. That's how we became a nation in fear for a few weeks in 1946.

On a some kind of day in 1974, I was editing a TV commercial in my office in Little Rock, and the phone rang. Someone shouted, "Charlie Pierce is on the phone!" I picked up the phone, "Hey, are you in town?"

"No, I'm in Texarkana and I'm going to make a new film. I wanted to run it by you."

"What's it called?"

"*The Town That Dreaded Sundown.*"

He didn't have to tell me what it was about. A beat, then Charlie spoke, "Do you think we can sleep at night, if I make it?" Even after all those years, I had to take a small, measured breath.

"Yeah, I believe we can sleep."

By then my childhood friend, "Charlie, the storyteller," had become an accomplished filmmaker, starting with the hugely successful *Legend of Boggy Creek.* Then *Bootleggers* was followed by

The Town That Dreaded Sundown, starring Academy Award winner Ben Johnson. It became a major success and a cult classic for him—plus, it was recently remade—a real tribute!

My Mother's Kitchen

MY EASIEST EARLY CHILDHOOD MEMORY IS OF MY MOTHER'S KITCHEN. Down a short hallway, I awakened to the smell of eggs and bacon as dawn was breaking. I could not only smell but also hear the sounds of eggs and bacon frying in her big cast-iron skillet. Early on, I took it as a sign that I was lucky to have my parents and to live in this house. Soon after waking up, I rolled out of bed and headed for the kitchen. Turning from the small gas stove, resting her egg turner on the skillet rim, Mom hugged me and said good morning. My dad, sitting at a large, chrome-legged, dove-gray Formica-topped table, folded the newspaper he was reading to give me a hug.

That table was the centerpiece of the kitchen. It was where every visitor ended up. The kitchen was floored with a dove-gray linoleum, and the walls wore a pink, flowery wallpaper. Mom was running a little ahead of the pink and gray period of the early 1950s.

That table was the de facto gathering place in our home. On

most days, friends or family occupied several of the chairs around that table, talking about what was going on in the world. Even at breakfast time, there was usually a relative or family friend who just came by to talk or enjoy scrambled eggs and bacon with my parents. Everyone was welcome.

⁓

The kitchen's one window looked toward the schoolyard across the street and admitted enough sunlight to illuminate the small porcelain sink. There—to help Mom out—I did my share of dishwashing in the early years, until relieved by my brother, Danny, who came along four years after I did.

Standing at the sink looking out on the schoolyard always made me feel good. Watching the happy activity on the grounds, everyone playing together, made me want to go to school.

On the wall of the kitchen was a painting of two young boys and a dog. Danny always believed it was us and our dog, Ted. Ted, a mixed breed—mostly bulldog—black with a white slash across his face—was with us until my late teenage years. I was heartbroken when he left us.

Even at the age of six, I was allowed to walk *alone* the half-mile downtown to Dad's grocery store because Ted accompanied me. Everybody along the way knew me and they knew Ted. Ted would literally stand in front of me at each street crossing until it was clear for me to cross. That behavior must have been instinctive because, as far as I know, my parents never taught him to monitor traffic. Ted was my ferocious defender—by my side almost every moment of every day.

I just couldn't get enough of the view through the kitchen window, which captured all of the activity on the school ground. Once, when I was five, I wandered onto the schoolyard at recess when all the children were outside playing. An older boy (a second-grader) started harassing me, saying I was a baby and should go away.

Loving being on the school grounds and disliking being called a baby, I didn't take the bullying well. I pushed the bully and turned away. When he grabbed me by the scruff of the neck and whirled me around, there were two of him! I had just had my first encounter with identical twins. I wrestled with one and Ted got the other by the jeans-leg, pulling him down and away from me. Quickly, the playground teacher grabbed all three of us and marched us toward the principal's office. Ted was shut outside and not happy about it. The teacher wanted the principal to discipline us. The principal (someone my parents knew, and I had seen at their grocery store) said that was fine, but he couldn't discipline the other two, because he couldn't discipline me.

"Why not?" the indignant teacher asked?

"Because he is only five years old and is not enrolled here," he laughed. "I see he has his dog with him." We all looked back to see Ted on his hind legs peeping through the upper glass half of the door. The principal told me to take Ted and cross the street to my house. He added that I probably shouldn't come on the school grounds during recess anymore.

Ted and I crossed the street to the house. Mother, said, "Where have you been? Outside playing?"

"Yes ma'am."

"Good, let's have some lunch." As far as I know, the principal never mentioned my escapade. Neither did I. Later, the twins and I became friends.

～

One of my earliest memories occurred in November of 1944, when I was four years old. Ted and I were playing on the kitchen floor, listening to my mother and several of my aunts discuss the horrors of WW II, which was then raging. Sitting around the table, nursing coffee cups held in two hands, they were discussing the danger they feared my Uncle Harold was in. He was near Bastogne, and they had read articles about the impenetrably thick forest in that area which might favor a German attack there. Over coffee, they concluded he might be safer than they thought. Mother, holding my two-month-old brother, Danny Harold Thomason in her arms, said she was glad she had made Uncle Harold's name a part of my brother's name. After eavesdropping on a conversation I really didn't understand, I was scared for Uncle Harold too.

Come December, we had already put up the small Christmas tree in the kitchen (we had a large one in the living room). Then I heard a reason to be really scared. Pretty much the same family members were around the table and they were terrified. I remember some tears. They believed Uncle Harold was still near the town of Bastogne, where the German army had mounted an attack through that "impenetrable thick forest," the Ardennes. The Germans were pushing toward Uncle Harold's position. The last major fight of the war in Europe, The Battle of the Bulge, was on!

I shouldn't have listened to the conversation, it worried me. I remember thinking about it each morning when I woke up. When I entered the kitchen, I asked if anybody had heard from Uncle Harold. Nobody had.

On the Saturday before Christmas, I went into the kitchen to find Mom looking out the window. She turned, gave me her usual hug, and said, "Here, let me help you up so you can see out the window." She lifted me to the countertop, and I looked toward the school. Daylight was just breaking, and a dusting of snow was falling. The school ground was full of tents, trucks, and soldiers. They had stopped late in the night and set up camp on their move toward the East Coast, heading for Europe. By now, the soldiers were stirring around, getting ready to fold their tents and move out. I immediately got Ted and headed once again to the school ground. The soldiers were very friendly, welcomed me, talked with me, patted me on the head, and asked if I wanted to go with them. They asked about Ted and told me he was a fine, great-looking dog. I felt good and headed back to the house. As I glanced at the kitchen window, I saw Mom smiling. She had observed it all.

An hour later, I stood outside in the slush as the convoy pulled out to parts unknown. I wonder what happened to that friendly bunch of young G.I.s who were kind to me and waved to me as their trucks headed down the street into history. It was a snowy, damp, cold day—a magnificent day as far as I was concerned.

Later, the family heard from Uncle Harold. He was safe. In May of 1945, I was playing in my room when I heard loud sounds coming from the kitchen. Following the sounds to their source, I found my mother and all my aunts laughing and hugging. "What's wrong Mom?" "Nothing's *wrong* son! Everything is *right!* The war in Europe is over! *All* your uncles will be coming home!"

I loved that kitchen, that table, that window.

Paddy

1951. IT WAS A COLD AND GRAY CHRISTMAS EVE IN SOUTH ARKANSAS. Although it rarely snowed there, a hint of frozen precipitation was in the air. Folks began to say that this might be the Christmas Eve when the song *White Christmas* becomes more than a dream in our part of the country.

My little brother Danny and I, bundled against the cold, played on the sidewalk near the house with our guard and always-faithful companion, Ted. Other people thought of him as a dog, but we knew him as our brother.

Danny first spotted Paddy wobbling down the sidewalk in front of Mr. Bigger's house—still the length of the high school away. "There he is!" We immediately put our plan into action and ran inside our house to the kitchen to find Mom.

I said, "Mom, Paddy is coming down the street and Danny wants us to give him a Christmas present!"

"Well, I think that is a fine thing for my boys to do!"

"But we don't have a gift and he's almost here," Danny said.

Mom always answered our questions about Paddy by saying it takes a lot to cover up memories past. She immediately walked to the Christmas tree in the living room, pulled a package from under the tree, gently removed the tag, and handed the package to my five-year-old brother, Danny. "Well, now you do."

～

We thanked her and ran back to the sidewalk. Paddy was just then passing the high school, a street away from us. We could see him plainly. He looked the same as he did every single day as he walked haltingly toward a bar downtown. Drunk. Always drunk. Even more so in the afternoon twilight as he staggered home. A gentle soul, he never failed to speak to us (or tip his hat to Mom when she was outside).

He crossed the street onto the sidewalk and passed us. "Morning, boys."

"Morning, Paddy." We could smell the booze when he got within five feet of us. "Danny and I wanted to give you a Christmas present." Paddy stopped. He turned, not understanding what I said. Danny tentatively put his hand out with the present, "Merry Christmas, Paddy."

Paddy stood there a moment, weaving slightly, trying to understand what just happened. "Huh?"

"It's a Christmas present—for you," Danny continued.

Paddy held the package, trying to focus his rheumy eyes on the red-and-green wrapping paper, the stick-on bow. "Really, for me?"

An awkward moment passed as we stood in silence. Finally,

Paddy pulled the ribbon and paper from the package, revealing a single pair of dark blue socks. Another moment passed before we saw tears form in his eyes. Danny eased closer to his big brother because this was not what we were expecting.

Tears streamed down Paddy's face. He mumbled a slurred "thanks," and continued his unsteady walk toward downtown and the bar. Danny and I did not know if we should feel joy or be upset. Paddy's tears caught us by surprise—such a tender act by a man so rough. Danny and I stepped back unconsciously, our brows furrowed. We turned to see Mother standing in the door. She flashed a small smile and headed back to the kitchen.

Soon the encounter was distant in our minds as we ran and played with our friend Charlie Pierce next door. Later, Woody Harrell came by on his pony, and we stroked the animal while speculating with him on whether it might snow today.

～

Night was falling, friends headed home, and we were about to head into the house when Ted signaled us with a soft bark. We looked toward town, and there he was in the twilight. Paddy. He was walking down the sidewalk carrying two white boxes almost the size of shoeboxes.

As he approached, we noticed that something was different. Now, from a distance of years, we might have been wrong, but it seemed he was walking a little straighter—maybe he was even a little taller. He stopped in front of us and smiled. In that moment, Paddy seemed unfamiliar. His ratty clothing was familiar, the constant stubble on his chin registered, but the smell of alcohol seemed somewhere between faint and nonexistent. He was definitely not as inebriated as he had been when he headed for town that morning.

"I bought you boys Christmas presents." He handed us each a box.

We eagerly opened them, finding the biggest collection of fireworks ever assembled. You name it—two-inch bombs, rockets, sparklers—if you can imagine it, it was there. Danny and I jumped in delight, almost spilling the contents of our boxes. "Thank you, Paddy! We love these!"

The tears started again and streamed down his face as he spoke, "I just can't believe, somebody loves old Paddy. Somebody loves dear old Paddy." He put his arms around us and hugged us. Then, holding his head a little steadier than usual, Paddy wiped the tears away and started on down the sidewalk. We boys would never admit it, but our eyes sort of watered up, too. Probably just the cold December air.

As we watched him walk away, I think it struck us why he smelled less of alcohol and walked a bit straighter. On that one day in 1951, he used his whiskey money to buy two little boys gifts ... Gifts we never forgot.

～

As we turned to go into the house, Danny said, "Did you see that?"

"See what?"

"A snowflake!"

"Really?" Soon, I saw them too, tiny snowflakes. Maybe that

white Christmas dream would come true!

The story didn't end there. I'm sure it had nothing to do with us, but we liked to think that the impromptu gift exchange helped start a chain of events. Soon, Paddy was no longer drinking. Before long, he had a job in our little town as a janitor at the Calhoun County Courthouse (a building on the National Historic Register of Historic Places). Over the years he advanced to become Head of Courthouse Maintenance. When he finally retired decades later, the mayor and the county judge signed proclamations declaring it Paddy Oliver Day in our hometown of Hampton. He deserved that day.

～

P.S. Many will already know this story because when my brother, Dr. Danny Thomason in Little Rock, decided to run Christmas radio commercials decades ago, he didn't promote his practice. Instead, he ran one-minute short stories of the true adventures of our bulldog brother, Ted, and us. We both are grateful for our family, our town, and the times in which we lived.

The Airplane

THE BRIGHT YELLOW BIPLANE WAS CIRCLING VERY TIGHT AND LOW—it's radial engine grumbling deeply. Charlie Pierce and I were lying in my front yard on a late summer day watching the plane. "I love airplanes," Charlie said with a sigh.

Mesmerized by the unusual sight, I could only reply, "Me too." We were bothered by the fact that we had never flown in a plane. We had never even stood close to one.

The plane finally drifted off toward the sunset, and we lay there silently on the cushion of green grass, enjoying the sundowner breeze that wafted over us.

After a few moments, Charlie spoke, "You know what we ought to do?"

"What?"

"We should build an airplane."

"What would we do for an engine?"

"We don't need one."

"What?" Charlie stood up and said, "I'll show you. Come

on!" I followed at a run, racing behind the shrubs that bordered our backyard and hid the pasture beyond. Charlie pointed to the barn that sort of straddled his backyard and mine, "See how the roof slants down steeply and then levels off over the stables?"

"Yeah?"

"So, we build it, pull it to the top of the barn. It gets fast as it goes down the steep tall part, and when it hits the level part of the stables, off we fly! We can land in the pasture where the horses are!"

I got it! To a ten-year-old like me, the plan made perfect sense! Plus, Charlie was a little older and it made sense to him, so it had to be good!

After scavenging for wood by breaking up old, discarded pallets, our materials acquisitions were nearly complete. The next morning, Charlie and I, plus our friends Sam, Max, Woody, and B.C., assembled near a stable with wood, metal, and tools borrowed from the Pierce workshop. We were building an airplane!

The blueprints were easy to follow because we had none. Never a worry about weight because the whole concept of gravity just confused us.

That afternoon, two older kids (high school students) came by on their way to baseball practice at the school next door. Victor Lee spoke, "What the hell are you boys doing?" Victor Lee was the only kid I knew who used "cuss" words.

"Building an airplane," Sam answered.

The other older kid, O.B., started laughing so hard he cried. Victor smiled, "Who is going to fly it?" The others informed them that Charlie and I were going to fly it. Max explained we planned to haul it to the top of the barn and launch it from there.

Victor Lee shook his head and smiled, "Well, fly by my house if you get a chance." O.B. just shook his head and they continued toward the baseball field.

After a couple of days, we were finished. Our "machine" did have the basic shape of an airplane. With two plank seats, broom handles to put your hands on while it flew, plus roller-skate landing gear nailed to the long plank that served as the fuselage, ours was a magnificent aircraft! Standing back to admire our design and smiling at each other in shared satisfaction, we were ready.

We all decided we had to wait to move it to the top of the barn until the next morning when our parents were gone, so they wouldn't delay our first flight with superfluous questions.

At mid-morning, everybody was ready for the flight. Our biggest problem was hauling the heavy contraption to the top of the tall barn. It took all of us to get it to the top and tied off by a rope that we looped over the barn and tied to a wooden post on the other side. The "plane" was hooked to the rope by a loose bowknot. The plan to start the flight was simple. You pull the rope, untying the bowknot, and freeing the "plane" to start its run down the steep part of the barn roof, and then you level out over the stables and head into the skies!

I was honored when Charlie decided I should be in the front seat and he would take the rear. Soon we were on our plank seats holding on to the broomstick handlebars and ready for launch.

On the ground, I saw Ted the dog, looking up at me with a, "You are a lunatic!" expression etched on his face.

The knot was pulled. The craft headed at breathtaking, rocket speed down the barn roof. Charlie, older and wiser, realizing how idiotic the plan was, rolled off the plane onto the tin roof of the barn. I, wind whipping across my face, continued solo. Speed increased dramatically. What excitement ... Sheer exhilaration!

Hitting the almost-horizontal portion of the roof covering the stables, I saw the beautiful blue sky ahead! In a blink, I left the roof and leaned back to take in the sky fully. For just a heartbeat ... our airplane actually flew. It seemed like a magnificently long time to me. In that split-second of weightlessness, treetops, housetops, church steeples, and my brothers-of-the-air, birds, were my only memories. For a moment I remember thinking, *I believe I will just buzz the school baseball field while I am up here!*

Then it was over, not in the long time it seemed to me, but in a nanosecond. Almost as soon as the heavy, wooden craft left the barn and briefly turned up toward the sky, it was plummeting back to earth. All I could see was the ground rushing toward me. I didn't even have time to scream before the plane's nose burrowed into the pasture beyond the stables. I was thrown headfirst into the ground. Blackness.

Consciousness did not return right away. Reality resumed sometime later, without my even having enjoyed dreamed replays of my exciting flight. My first conscious awareness was of hearing voices. Sight came later and pain slowly caught up. My friends were standing over me. Sam Oliver was whispering, "Is he dead?"

"No, I'm not dead! What are you saying that for?" Ted was standing by me, too disgusted to even lick my face.

Charlie was apologizing for bailing out on me, "Sorry, just thought I was going to make it too heavy."

I became aware that my nose was bleeding. A small cut on my head was also bleeding. B.C. and Max lifted me by the armpits and tested my legs. Wobbly. They helped me learn to walk again. Finally, Charlie asserted that I could walk on my own and we turned to inspect the damage to our "plane." She was in pieces. An airship whose experimental days were over, she would never fly again.

I was okay, just a bloody nose, a bump on my forehead, and a small cut on my temple. As the story was told and retold after school started that fall, I flew further and further, higher and higher, and was near death when they rescued me from the smoldering crash scene. In more colorful versions, the aircraft burned.

It was my first flight, but it wouldn't be my last. I never lost my love of airplanes. In my twenties, I got my flight license, and I still love the feeling of lifting off from the earth. My first flight—in a boy-built wooden airplane—makes me a safer pilot because I am always ready for a repeat of that first flight. I have had, over the years, two flights that ended with silent engines but both with better results than that long-ago first flight.

The Foxhole

In this story, I will refer to the enemy combatant as "Scut Farkus," a character from the movie Christmas Story. *No, our Scut Farkus was not really a bully but it just makes for a shorthand way to tell a story. Plus, I'm not sure our real friend would have wanted me to use his name.*

IT WAS A CRISP FALL SATURDAY MORNING IN SOUTH ARKANSAS and the leaves were just beginning to change. I woke up early and was in the front yard playing with Ted. Soon, my third-grade classmate, Woody Harrell, showed up on his bike. In later life, he would drop the nickname "Woody" and take his given name, Searcy. Named for his father, a highly successful banker, he would go on to become even more successful as an attorney, investor, and owner of multiple banks and businesses throughout the country.

Soon my next-door friend, Charlie Pierce (of childhood aviation fame), showed up and even sooner we were all bored. Charlie suggested, "Let's go across the street, play war, and dig a foxhole."

Sounded good to us! Grabbing a couple of shovels and our BB guns, we crossed the street to a vacant lot and began digging in the soft soil. As the hole grew deeper, we piled the shoveled dirt around the edge. Soon, we could stand in the hole and be almost enveloped by the earth. A pretty good foxhole, if we said so ourselves!

We settled into the damp hole and traded WWII stories about our fathers and uncles. Our little troop sat, waiting—BB guns ready—for the "enemy" to attack. We were about to get a bit more than we bargained for.

"Uncle Harold was in the Battle of the Bulge," I was saying, when suddenly I was interrupted by the distant pop of enemy fire and the zing of a bullet passing just over our heads! What?! There was no real enemy!

"What the hell?" Charlie shouted. Playing soldier was one of the few occasions when we could use restricted "soldier words," and this was one of them.

Woody whispered, "Sure sounded like a gunshot." As if in confirmation, another POP sounded and another bullet whistled overhead! Damn! No doubt—we were under full-out attack! We grabbed our BB guns. Instead of standing up and firing, we hugged the bottom of the foxhole. We were young, not stupid!

Then ... Silence. Finally, Woody slowly raised his head and peeped over the edge. POW! Thump! Dirt was flying everywhere, and Woody piled back on top of us! We didn't know if we should run or start screaming for our mothers. Tears. We were all near tears.

Using a soldier word, Charlie's cracking voice asked, "Did you see who the hell it is?"

Woody replied, "It's Scut. He's in the ditch beside the street!" Scut Farkus was a high school student. We had even less use for high school students than they had for us. POP! Zing! Another bullet whizzed overhead!

Hyperventilating, I managed to mutter, "What's he doing?" Woody replied, "He's laughing." Another shot rang out and thumped into the dirt above our heads. We hugged each other tighter. Above our sniffles, we all could hear Scut's laughter.

In the distance, an elderly lady's voice echoed across the open land, "Young man, leave those children alone!" Scut answered with another shot and more laughter. This guy was having fun! We burrowed deeper into the moist floor of our foxhole.

An eternity passed before we heard a car's tires squeal as a vehicle rounded the corner from the highway to the side street nearest us. Could it be General Patton's troops to the rescue just like they saved Uncle Harold at the Battle of the Bulge?

No. It was better! It was Calhoun County Sheriff Doyle B. Duncan. We raised our heads just in time to see the sheriff snatch Scut from the ditch and lift him high into the air by the scruff of his neck. Scut's rifle flew through the air. The sheriff shouted, "What the heck are you doing, boy?" I guess he was not allowed to use soldier words. We stood up to observe the rout, holding our BB guns, smiling through our tears. Sheriff Duncan shouted, "You boys okay?"

A chorus: "Yes, sir."

He dragged Scut toward the squad car, yelling back to us, "Okay, great! Have a good morning."

Standing shoulder-to-shoulder like choirboys, we replied in unison, "Yes, sir."

Now, I know you are thinking, I guess you boys had to give statements and testify against Scut at his trial for attempted murder. Did the *Dallas Morning News* actually send a sketch artist to portray Woody on the witness stand? Wonder how long Scut was incarcerated? Did he get his GED while behind bars?

That's not the way the sword of justice worked in Hampton.

As we walked across the lot toward the street, the sheriff yanked off his heavy leather belt, and WHAP ... It landed on Scut's butt. "Boy, the next time you do something like that, I will come for you!" WHAP! Scut tried to hold back the tears, his legs still dangling in mid-air. WHAP! The sheriff put him down then spoke softly, "Now take your rifle and get to your house—and don't leave it again today!"

"Yes, sir," Scut grabbed his rifle and ran up the hill.

～

I finally walked back into the house to be greeted by Ted and my brother Danny.

Mom was preparing lunch. She glanced at me, "Hey, did you guys have fun this morning?"

"We did ... Lots of fun!"

～

Scut was just shooting to scare us and amuse himself on a slow Saturday morning. Nonetheless, when someone's bullets are scattering dirt in your face, you tend to get scared—especially, when you are nine years old. Today, Scut would probably have been incarcerated. Who knows how it would turn out in today's hyper-vigilant age? Scut could end up a hardened criminal. Using the Sheriff Duncan method, Scut went home and continued his life. We saw him in the schoolyard on Monday and all was normal. As an adult, he became a successful businessman in a larger community. As far as I know, he never shot at another person. And if he did, I know it was all in fun.

The Great Watermelon Heist

THIS STORY IS FROM LONG AGO. I'm not going to tell all the names involved because I might get somebody into trouble yet!

It was a perfect South Arkansas summer night. Having just graduated from Hampton High School, I was attending a party with a group of another high school's graduates who lived in the "big city" of Camden, twenty miles west of my small hometown of Hampton. As I bashfully made my way into the party where I knew few other attendees, the record player spun The Platters' *Twilight Time*. The girls from Camden looked worldly, sophisticated in their brightly-colored party dresses. Life was good. Real good.

Soon, Ann Burns, clearly the leader of the pack, approached me. A stunning beauty with sparkling eyes, flaming red hair, and the swagger of captain of the Camden Panther cheerleaders, she studied me for a moment before speaking. She and her friends, "had always heard that stealing watermelons from a farmer's field was a great thrill," though she couldn't imagine why.

After a moment during which I mustered the best baritone possible at age seventeen-and-a-half, I asked if she and her friends wanted to try it.

"Yes, tonight."

I wasn't sure what to do until I made a long distance, collect phone call to a classmate back in Hampton. The adventure was underway. Shortly, three of my classmates plus Ann and three of her friends piled into one car.

We traveled back to Hampton and then along a narrow, gravel, country road on a night that was so black Ann finally remarked, "This place is so dark they must have to pump daylight in!" If you have always lived in metropolitan areas, it is hard to imagine what "dark" is really like. And in those days, Camden, Arkansas, was so metropolitan that it had two movie theaters.

Conway Twitty's *It's Only Make Believe* wafted from the radio as we came upon a large field and stopped. Moving silently (except for an occasional nervous giggle from Ann and her friends) to a rickety barbwire fence, we pushed it down so the girls could wiggle their party dresses across intact.

I can't explain why it was such an adrenalin rush to steal a couple of watermelons that might have cost seventy-five cents at the time—but it was. If you didn't overdo it, the farmers usually couldn't care less. Every day, crows ate more melons than we were about to take. Plus, any farmer would have gladly given us all the melons we wanted, had we merely knocked on his door and asked politely.

Soon, we were deep into the large field, lit only by the

occasional firefly, picking dusty melons and snapping them from the vine. Ann whispered in my ear, "You're right, I still don't know why, but this is exciting!"

Laden with our booty—six small melons—and transfixed by the sight of the girls in party dresses, tip-toeing their prizes across a farmer's field, we small-town boys had never been happier. The parked car was just ahead.

Suddenly, a bright light swept across us and shouts filled the air.

"I'm tired of you people stealing my melons!" a coarse voice shouted.

Another voice, surly and cocksure, followed, "You're gonna pay!"

Sudden, blinding flashes followed by eardrum-shattering reverberations filled the air. Bursts of noise and orange flashes seemed to be all around us. Shotguns!

Dropping my watermelon and grasping my right side, I went down, screaming, "Run, I'm hit!" From our left and right, the air was filled with screaming, crying voices, gunfire, and flashes. Ann and one of her friends plunged into the dark woods. Through the melee, I heard Ann telling her friend she was afraid of snakes.

One of her friends shouted, "Ann, snakes are not your biggest problem at the moment!"

One of my friends and another of the Camden girls sprinted for the car. A new blast of gunfire lit up the sky and my friend fell. The terrified girl ran through a barbwire fence, shredding her beautiful party dress. I heard a car door slam. The car roared to life and took off, the spinning tires throwing up a cascade of dust and gravel.

Then, complete and eerie silence. I saw the menacing beams of flashlights sweeping through the darkness. Suddenly, I heard the car again as it made a noisy, honking, dramatic return with Ann's friend crying and shouting, "Ann! Ann! Please—where are you?"

The flashlights immediately swept toward the car. Ann and her friend, party dresses tattered from bushes and barbwire, burst from the woods and flew into the car. Another blast of gunfire and suddenly a man stood in front of the car with his rifle leveled toward my Hampton friend, the driver. The other gunman stuck his gun in the window and repeated, "Somebody's gonna pay!"

What happened next is why anybody who has Ann Burns Hoy as a friend is lucky. Amid the chaos and hysteria, she shoved the door into the gunman's face and hopped out screaming. She snatched the gun from him. The guy was shocked. Ann grew stronger, "I'll pay for every damn watermelon in the damn field but you are going to let us get these people to a hospital, right now!" Her friends were by then out of the car and standing shoulder-to-shoulder with her.

A beat. The guy stared at her a moment then mumbled, "O.K."

⁓

By then, I was back to the car and—even though already ashamed—I could not suppress the laughter any longer. As the "farmer" and his "hired man" also broke into laughter, the distraught girls became silent and wondered what the hell was wrong with us.

I moved closer to Ann and told her.

The "farmer" and "hired man," the shotguns and search-lights ... it was all a hoax. We boys were all in on it. We had treated the "big city" Camden girls to a bit of impromptu, home-spun drama. The gunfire was all blanks (but what large flames!). My wound? I was fine, just wearing a little ketchup on my shirt. There was a tense moment as the girls worked out their feelings. Would they release the tension in laughter? Start crying again? Or pronounce derision on their country-bumpkin enactors?

Ann looked at me for a moment, her eyes sparkling even more. She slapped me so hard across the face I saw stars and stum-bled backward. Her blow had landed with such force that my eyes watered. She did the right thing, giving her friends a chance to laugh—and it was over. Things settled down and we introduced the "farmer" and "hired hand" as high school friends of ours.

Ann's friend said, "Well, I'm going to take the damn water-melon home, anyway." Her father kept it in their refrigerator for several weeks—making a show of displaying it, telling guests the story of "The Great Watermelon Heist." That was certainly better than suing us. As I recall, we boys did have the decency to volun-teer to pool our money and pay for the damaged dresses.

As the years passed, my friends and I regretted that we did such a foolish thing. Afterward, we confined ourselves to less exciting exploits during our free time (not entirely true, more later). After all these years, the one lesson that I took away from that night is that if I were in a war, I would want those fearless women with me! I hope they all forgave us for that night of terror. My hope is that even they look back on that night from this distance as an adventure—though one you only want to experience once in a lifetime.

Ann Burns Hoy became a beloved and esteemed educator at Trinity School in New York City. I'm sure all of her students, who went on to become warriors on Wall Street and nattily-attired sharks in banks never would have imagined that long ago, Ann was also a veteran of warfare, even if it was a war of watermelons conducted on fields of fire illuminated most nights, not by gunfire, but armies of lightning bugs.

The Soldier Beside the Road

ONE OF MY CLOSEST CHILDHOOD FRIENDS, Jerry Stringfellow, was at the wheel. I was riding shotgun as we rolled through the hills of Kentucky on a hot, humid, July night long ago. The sky was filled with flashing lightning and intermittent rain. The clock just hit twelve a.m. and the famed rock station, WAKY, Louisville, Kentucky, with great fanfare, dropped the needle on Elvis Presley's newest release, *Teddy Bear*, for the first time.

A flash of lightning revealed someone on the shoulder of the road ahead. Jerry saw him, "A hitchhiker in the middle of nowhere, should we stop for him?"

"Let's do."

Each summer, we made our way from Arkansas to Kentucky—thumbs out, hitchhiking, hoping some good soul would carry us closer to our destination. We knew what it was like to be in the middle of nowhere in the middle of the night.

Two high school kids from South Arkansas, we had summer jobs with a giant roofing company out of Louisville. The boss, a friend of our parents, trusted us more than he should have. We were seventeen years old and driving a huge truck carrying a construction crane. Tonight, we were relocating a giant crane in our giant truck to a new project in Cleveland, Ohio—three hundred-fifty miles away.

All summer we would move around the Midwest, roofing everything from Churchill Downs to Ford Motor Company. The work was unbelievably hot and hard. So hot, we went to work at four a.m. We had to quit by noon when the heat was so intense the roof would begin to melt and stick to our feet. It was tough work. We liked the job because it kept us in shape to report back to football practice in Hampton in August of each summer. We had to be in shape for football because Bear Bryant, the Alabama football legend, had related in a newspaper interview that our high school coach, Boyd Arnold, was the toughest guy he had ever known. Coach Bryant knew what he was talking about. Ironically, because he *was* so tough on us, we all loved Coach Arnold!

Jerry slowed the truck to a stop and the hitchhiker with his worn duffel bag made his way to the truck. I opened the passenger door and he crawled up into the cab, immediately filling it with the smell of booze and tobacco. I noticed the lettering on his windbreaker—U.S. Marines, Quantico, Virginia. "I like your jacket," I said.

"Thanks, had it since boot camp, thought I might get rained on."

I replied, "I like it, and if you ever wanna' get rid of it, I'll take it!"

"I hear you, my name is Jimmy." He offered his hand and we shook it.

We rolled on through the seemingly endless night, talking. Jimmy had served in Korea as a U.S. Marine but didn't seem to have much inclination to tell two naïve teenagers about his war. It became obvious that the war had affected him greatly. He talked about the many Veterans Administration hospitals with which he was well-acquainted. He asked us about our families. We told him—all good things about all good people. We got almost nothing back except that he grew up in West Virginia and hadn't been home since he left for Korea.

Looking much older than his thirty-one years, he'd been a drifter since his discharge. Jimmy thought he might go to California someday because, as he said, "California is always warm and I'm always cold."

Jerry asked if he was looking for a job.

"Nobody's gonna' hire me."

"Why?"

"I'm just plain worthless."

∽

"That's crazy," our supervisor, J.B., also from our hometown, muttered as we stood on the Ohio job-site. "You two are suckers for every sad story you hear." He glanced at the truck where Jimmy was napping. "You f**king guys will be the death of me yet."

"Does that mean he has a job?"

"Damn it, get settled into the boarding house and I'll see

you in the morning. Bring him, but he won't last a week."

The "boarding house" concept has been around forever, the forerunner of B&B's. We settled into a room with two single beds and got Jimmy the only room available—the size of a closet with a folding bed.

When we rolled out of our beds at 3:15 a.m., Jimmy was standing in the hallway waiting for us. At the site, J.B. threw Jimmy a set of gloves and assigned him one of the toughest jobs of all, as a "hot"carrier. Hot tar would be pumped to the top of the ten-story building and Jimmy would have to carry heavy, five-gallon cans of the boiling hot liquid to the guys installing the roofing material. If you moved too fast, it splashed on you and inflicted painful burns. If you moved too slowly, the foreman screamed at you that the tar was cooling and becoming useless.

Jerry and I thought he might not even make it through the first day as he worked through his hangover, sweating profusely and breathing heavily. At noon, quitting time, we asked, "How'd you make it?"

"Better than being shot at by the damn Chinese and North Koreans—but not by f**king much." J.B. glanced at us and mouthed, "He won't be back."

The next morning, Jimmy was waiting in the hall again. That's how it went all week. Even J.B.'s admiration grew as Jimmy seemed to get stronger each day. On Thursday, Jimmy announced that he was totally giving up drinking because between Korea and drinking he had become "worthless."

That night, he stood in the hallway as we told our mothers

on the pay phone that we loved them and would see them in August, in time for football practice. Afterward, as we walked toward a White Castle for dinner, Jimmy said he wished he could talk to his mother.

"Why don't you?"

He softly replied, "Because I'm worthless."

～

Friday noon. Payday. We were all paid extremely well, and Jimmy was no exception. When he saw the check, his eyes got wide.

J.B. looked at us and whispered, "He made it a week but now that he has money, he won't be back."

Offended, we said we would have him there on Monday morning at 4 a.m. sharp.

That night, we went to a movie, *The 3:10 to Yuma*, starring Glenn Ford. Then back to the boarding house. We finally had a chance to sleep late.

In the pre-dawn hours, we heard a soft knock as our door opened, "Buddy, you guys awake?"

"We are now."

Jimmy ambled into the room all hangdog and sat on the edge of Jerry's bed. He might have been drinking. His clothes always reeked of beer and alcohol anyway, so he might not have been drinking. Damned if we could tell. "I called my momma," he said softly.

Jerry grinned, "Great! And did she say you were worthless?"

"No."

"What did she say?"

"She said she loved me ... and missed me." In the dim light, we saw his eyes glisten.

"That's great."

"Yeah," Jimmy replied as he stood, moved to the door and paused, "yeah, that's real good." He walked out. We had trouble going back to sleep.

We slept in. Finally, we opened the door for breakfast and noticed something hanging on the doorknob. It was the Quantico Marine jacket I loved. Hanging out of the pocket was a folded piece of paper. Reluctantly, Jerry unfolded it and I read aloud, "Sorry, going home." That was it, nothing else.

∼

Monday. "Today, because we are shorthanded, Mr. Stringfellow and Mr. Thomason will be the "hot" carriers." The crew laughed as J.B. finished.

We stood, put our feet onto the twelve-inch weights at the bottom of the crane cables, grabbed the cable and hung on for dear life to be rapidly hoisted to the top of the ten-story building in silence and defeat. As we jumped from the crane to the top of the building (yes we had to jump three feet to the rooftop), J.B. finally spoke, "Well, boys, you did the right thing. Charity just doesn't always work out ... But you always have to try."

I wore that Marine jacket for years in respect of all the other "Jimmys" crisscrossing the blue highways of our country, trying to find their way home after a war.

∼

Jerry became a respected physician in our home state, and I became a high school football coach before drifting into the film business. We could never decide if Jimmy was drunk that night. I like to think he wasn't.

I always imagine his mother looking out of her kitchen window as the sun rises over her West Virginia home. Suddenly, she sees her son start up the long path to her house. Her eyes well up with tears. The dishrag she is holding falls on the dog's head. The screen door slams behind her as she breaks into a run to embrace her little boy, Jimmy—the prodigal son.

I never met Jimmy's momma, but that's how I see it whenever I remember Jimmy.

Mistake at Calion Lake

ON A LATE SATURDAY AFTERNOON, my friend, Bob Biggers, and I decided to do what a lot of 11th (me) and 12th-graders (him) did in my hometown in the Fifties. We decided to head for Fordyce, the nearest town north, and cruise Main Street enough times to assess the active female presence. Then we would head southwest for the next town, Camden, where—ever hopeful—we repeated the procedure. On the final leg, we headed southeast toward El Dorado to cruise the courthouse square and the popular drive-in before retreating to our native Hampton around midnight. Most times, on our Saturday night ritual, we circumscribed a triangle of seventy-five miles, without sighting any unattached teenage females who suited our fancy.

On the day that I have in mind, we were doing it in style, as Bob's mother just bought a brand new Buick. We couldn't believe she was letting Bob drive her "dreamboat" for the night. Soon, we were in Fordyce, drinking chocolate shakes at a drive-in, listening to The Platters and Chuck Berry on the jukebox, and catching up with fellow high school students.

Then we pointed the powerful Buick toward a bigger, more exciting population of teenage beauties. In twenty-five minutes, we arrived in Camden, where we headed for the most popular hangout in town, The Duck Inn. There, we saw friends, including Ann Burns, who I had a crush on and whom I had earlier subjected to the watermelon raid (but she had started speaking to me again!). Unfortunately, she was with her boyfriend.

We bumped into the all-star Camden quarterback, Lanny Shofner, who decided to join us for the rest of the trip—to El Dorado and back to Hampton. Soon we three were on our way, and in twenty-five minutes (it was twenty-five minutes to each town on the wagon wheel trip) we were in El Dorado at the local hangout. Bob, Lanny, and I alternated in trying to impress the lovely Donna Axum. Having exhausted our wits without any sign of immediate reward, we then headed for Hampton around eleven-thirty.

～

That's when the trip went bad. Very bad.

On a narrow two-lane highway near the small lumber mill town of Calion, we passed a truck in our polished green and white Buick. As soon as we got around him, the driver started blinking his bright lights furiously. We turned off the main highway to go to Calion Lake and the guy turned with us. Bob sped up. The guy sped up.

Lanny said, "I don't know what this guy's problem is, but he seems to want a piece of us." We knew it was one guy and three of us and by now we were irritated by the guy's provocations.

Bob said, "Yeah, if he wants to mess with us, we'll take him on."

I blustered, "Yeah, he picked the wrong guys to mess with!"

We were at the lake, where a long, circular one-way street routed traffic around the lakeshore cabins. We took it. Lanny glanced back, "Damn, the S.O.B. is taking the wrong way! He is going to block us!" The full fight-or-flight thing was working a moment later as we found ourselves facing his oncoming head-lights. We slowed down, and so did the threatening truck, its high-beams blinding us. Soon we were stopped on the narrow pavement with the vehicles head-to-head. We were only a couple of feet apart.

Lanny quipped, "Okay boys, get your watches and jackets off, we have to attend to a little business here."

⌒

As we started taking the gear off, I murmured, "We shoulda stayed a little longer in El Dorado."

"We should just kick the rear end of whoever this is ..." was the last thing I heard anyone in the car say, as the guy leapt from his truck. Suddenly the windshield of the beautiful new Buick was in a million pieces, peppering us with glass and causing minute specks of red stuff to appear on our faces.

We sat stunned as the barrel of a high caliber rifle came through the space where the windshield used to be. "Get out and line up beside the car or I will kill all three of you sons-a-bitches."

As the killer prodded us with the rifle barrel, Lanny managed to say that we might be in a little trouble. That's right, and I said "killer" because by now I had figured out that those specks of red stuff on our faces were blood from glass-shard wounds—and that we were going to see a whole bunch more of it!

We stood beside the car in front of a guy who seemed about six-feet-four and probably two hundred and fifty pounds.

The rifle looked even larger than he did. The big man resumed swearing—a spitted barrage consisting mostly of the very words our daddies had specifically instructed us to never use—complemented by menacing postures and flaming eyeballs. He ordered us to kneel down beside the car. Bob started laughing, a quiet laugh but a laugh. The guy, who seemed to think I was the one laughing, shouted, "I will kill you first, you bastard."

We were now kneeling on the ground as he kept shouting at us and putting the rifle to our faces. Hey, we were doing well! We weren't screaming. We weren't even sniveling with runny noses... Yet. "Whose damn car it this?" We didn't say a word. He stared at us for what seemed an eternity.

Finally, Bob whispered, "It's mine ... sir."

The soon-to-be-killer, spoke, "Well, I'm gonna ..." Before he could finish, he stopped because we all heard it.

Sirens. Across the open flatland—probably a mile away—we could see the red lights of a speeding police car that had nowhere to be going other than right to us. Bob, Lanny, and I studied it for a moment before the killer spoke unbelievable words, "Okay, let's just forget this happened. I'm leaving ... Don't say anything or I will come back for you."

We believed him. The big man jumped in his Chevrolet truck, spun it around, and headed out on the one-way street. As we watched in shock and disbelief, he drove back to the main road, waited casually as the police car roared past him, then turned the other way and disappeared into the night.

∼

The lights in cabins around the lake were beginning to come on now. Curtains were cautiously drawn aside. Bob spoke first, "What the heck am I going to tell my mom? Hell, I can't hang around with you guys anymore. You are too damn dangerous!"

The police car pulled up. Hefting his gun belt with both hands, the deputy lumbered from his car, surveyed the broken windshield, looked at the specks of blood on our faces, and spoke, "Something going on here?"

A beat, then Lanny said, "Yes sir, a man in a Ford truck was trying to throw a rock into the lake and he accidentally hit my car."

"Did he pay you for breaking the windshield?"

"No sir, but he left his phone number and said, he would send a check whenever we could tell him the amount," Lanny lied.

I'm thinking, I hope this guy doesn't ask for the phone number. The deputy asked a few more questions but seemed to lose interest in the driver of the "Ford" truck. Then, focusing on our predicament, he surmised, "Well, it's going to be windy driving home," and left.

Lights in the neighboring cabins began to go out. Crickets

and bullfrogs resumed their mating calls, the only sounds intruding on the rural nighttime silence and the void around us. Then Bob asked, to no one in particular, "What am I going to tell my mother?"

We started driving the sixteen miles home. We were silent. It was windy.

I didn't ask what Bob told his mother, but I would know two weeks later when I was home alone in the late afternoon and there was a soft knock at the door. I pulled the door open and there he stood—the guy that threatened to kill us! He was even bigger and scarier than I remembered.

"You're Harry, right?" I see a pistol strapped to his waist and my knees buckle.

The words, "Yes sir, are you going to shoot me?" escape my lips.

"I know you are here alone, and I wanted to talk to you." My heart rate doubled and he saw my discomfort, "I just wanted to explain why I did what I did."

"That's okay, sir. You don't have to explain." As I started to slowly close the door, he stuck his massive arm out and held it.

"Some guy's been messing around with my wife. He drives that same car. I was a little drunk the other night, and I figured I would do some damage to him—teach him a lesson. I didn't realize you guys were so young. I'm sorry."

"That's okay, sir."

"No, it's not. I need to pay for your buddy's windshield, and I don't know where he lives. I can leave you a check if you will find out what I owe."

Having decided he's not going to kill me, I said, "Let me call him first and I will tell you where he lives." I went to the hallway phone and called Bob's house. He answered.

As my words tumbled out, Bob freaked out, "No, don't send him over here!"

"Bob, he's not going to kill us!'

Bob answered, "I told my mother we were in the movie and we came out and found the windshield shattered. The insurance company has already fixed it and I can't change the story now! He can't come over here."

I got it, I understood. No need for more trouble. I walked back to the front door and broke the news to the gunman. "Okay, but here is my phone number if he wants me to pay for it. I'm sorry for the trouble."

As he walked away, I summoned the courage to speak, "Sir, I don't want to be nosy but why do you have the gun on?"

He spun around on the sidewalk and his expression softened. "Oh, I'm a deputy sheriff in Union County. That's how I found you." What? Then the middle-aged deputy sheriff of Union County who had recently nearly killed my buddies and me stepped into his car and drove away as casually as if he had been delivering the newspaper.

Months later, my mother let me borrow her new car because I had a date in El Dorado, the county seat of Union County. Just past Calion, the first hamlet after the county line, I was thinking about the summer evening ahead and didn't notice as my speed slipped a little over the limit. Soon, the piercing sound of a siren interrupted my reverie. Checking the rear view-mirror, I saw a sheriff's car behind me. As I slowed down, the vehicle with the flashing lights pulled alongside me. At the wheel was the same deputy.

He stared at me for a moment. Finally, I saw a glint of recognition flash across his face. He smiled almost shyly, gave me a thumbs up, and motioned for me to go. As I did, the accelerator in Mom's car seemed hesitant to reach anything close to the speed limit. The deputy fell in behind me, then finally disappeared from my rear-view mirror.

∼

Note: Donna Axum mentioned in the story later became Miss America 1964.

The Great Snowball

UNLIKE WITH OUR FRIENDS FURTHER NORTH, THE RARE SNOWSTORM in south Arkansas was a cause of effusive celebration ... A spontaneous holiday. People got excited and rushed to the grocery stores, buying enough milk, bread, eggs, and bacon to feed their families for a month. No community within four hundred miles had enough snow plows and salt to clear the streets, highways, and country roads. Two inches of snow was enough to cancel school. The welcome break in routine just lasted a day, long enough for a celebration. One afternoon's sunshine was usually enough to melt the snow and bring a return to the humdrum schedule.

It was an unusually cold day right after Thanksgiving when my roommate, Don Henson, and another friend, Wayne Freppon, walked out of Cross Hall, the jock dorm at Southern Arkansas University where we, as football players, resided. Our destination was breakfast in the cafeteria. Wayne noticed it first, "It's snowing!" It was a rare occasion for South Arkansas—especially in November.

By the time we came out of the cafeteria, the ground was covered. Other students were beginning to toss snowballs the size of golf balls. Everybody was laughing and ebullient. It was like Christmas had arrived early!

That night, we left the dorm for the fieldhouse to burn off some energy. Amazingly, the snow was still falling steadily. Probably ten inches of snow covered the ground. It was enough, we figured, to cancel classes for two, maybe three days. We played basketball and worked out on the trampolines for a couple of hours. We headed back to Cross Hall, plodding through the snow, freezing as the temperature hung in the low twenties.

Don Ragar, another athlete, noticed it first.

There was a commotion among the residents of Graham Hall, a dormitory that we always had considered the "rich kids" dorm, though years later I realized that was not an apt description. Peering through the falling snow, we could see twenty or so guys from the dorm scrambling around outside.

After a moment, Ragar grasped what they were doing. "They're building a f**king snowball. A big snowball!" As we trudged closer through the heavy snow, it came into focus—they were piling snow up by the bucket and molding it into the largest snowball we had ever seen! Hell, no one in our group had probably ever seen a snowball over four or five inches in diameter. This round blob was already over six feet tall and getting bigger by the minute!

"Why are you guys doing this?" Henson, asked.

One of them shouted back, "We're gonna make some

money!"

"How?" Freppon wanted to know.

"We are going to make it ten feet high and then we are going to sell chances starting tomorrow on when it will be totally melted, no snow left. Whoever is closest gets seventy-five percent of the pot. We get twenty-five."

"How much are the chances?" Freppon again.

"Two dollars," came the reply.

The next day was bitterly cold and gray. As we left Cross Hall for the cafeteria, we detoured enough to look across campus toward Graham Hall. There it was, truly a thing of beauty—a ten-foot-tall snowball!

⟶

In the cafeteria, we observed the boys from Graham Hall moving from table to table selling chances on what date the snowball would melt. Ragar inquired, "How are sales?"

"Great! We are easily gonna' top thirty-five hundred. Everybody is buying multiple tickets."

That night, we did something we never got to do. In the unusual cold, a small lake on campus had frozen over. According to our teammate, Loren Partain, the ice was a foot thick. We figured twelve inches of ice would easily support a car. So, we all piled into Henson's car and headed for the lake. Ragar suggested we find the public radio station that played classical music and turn the volume way up. We did so and soon Henson drove the car at high speed onto the shallow lake and hit the brakes so that the car spun like a ballerina over the ice to the chords of Mr.

Handel's *Water Music*. Hitting the gas produced another spin and slide as the Chevy Bel Aire glided to the music. Most of us in the car probably didn't appreciate classical music, but that night—as a car full of jocks glided and spun across the lake—it all seemed appropriate.

Finally, Ragar broke the silence, "We should try to win that pot of money. We need to buy some chances."

Freppon said, "It's supposed to stay cold for a while, we would just be throwing away our money."

"I've got a plan," Ragar assured us. He always had a plan.

We were up most of the night. I kept searching for long-term weather reports on my transistor radio. Henson was checking the melt rate of ice at given temperatures. In those days, there was no Internet, but someone had a set of encyclopedias. We also gathered various science books. Ragar was calling a friend in Vegas to access the odds of how many days we should bet on. We went to our close friend, the resident jock-dorm brainy student and super athlete, Larry "Loco" McNeil, to assemble all of the data into a report. Actually, it was good science-work for a bunch of jocks!

By morning, girded by the impressive array of assembled facts, we were ready to take action. Ragar bought tickets on twenty different days that Partain determined from all the info would be the most likely days under certain conditions for the ten-foot snowball to disappear. We then went back to the routine of campus life and waited.

When the first of the seven dates arrived six days later and the weather had remained unseasonably cold, the snowball didn't appear any smaller at all. We weren't worried, we still had nine dates to go and they weren't consecutive. A long stretch of slightly warmer weather ensued. Partain slipped down during the night and measured the height of the snowball. It was only nine feet tall.

A week later it was six feet tall. Partain believed we were cutting it close but that we would be about right on one of our last dates. We calculated that our share of the winnings would be over three thousand dollars. Almost everybody else had picked dates which had already passed. We were sitting pretty!

When the snowball was five feet tall, the weather turned cold again. The snowball seemed to have taken on a life of its own. It refused to melt, or so it seemed. When an overnight snowfall left an inch of new snow on campus trees, it was rumored that the Graham Hall boys might have packed snow back onto the ball. We were reminded that, if no one got within a week of the melt date, they got to keep all of the pot.

Having exhausted our research—and disappointed in our combined logic—we gave in to full-blown panic. It was one week until Christmas break and the damn snowball seemed stronger than ever! Everybody involved crammed into our dorm room for a hastily called, emergency meeting. The next Sunday was one of the last three dates we had selected. Something had to be done.

Partain knew a guy in Nelson Hall, the dorm next door, who would implement his plan for ten dollars. Freppon and Henson asked Partain what the plan was. "Okay, there's a guy in Nelson Hall who has exhibited arsonist tendencies in the past ..."

Ragar jumped in, "What the hell do you mean, 'arsonist tendencies'?"

"Well, I think he might have burned some things before—nothing major." Ragar shook his head as Partain continued, "I 'suggested' he take gasoline, drench the snowball and set it on fire."

Henson replied, "If we burn it will that disqualify us?"

"No, they didn't spell that out—they'd have to give us the money. This is why I want to use the guy from Nelson Hall. What can go wrong? Besides, they're not going to know we did it ... And we believe they cheated. They deserve it!" Nobody spoke.

～

Somewhere close to one-thirty in the morning, a guy dressed in black scurried low across the campus, headed for the snowball. A few lights were still on in Graham Hall as the guy cleaved footholds into the softened snowball and climbed to the top. He drenched it with the ten gallons of gasoline he hoisted up, and then he climbed down.

Back at Cross Hall, we moved slowly through the door and walked into the darkness to peer toward the dorm.

After a moment, a gigantic fireball exploded from the snowball and flames shot several stories into the air. It was a magnificent sight! Immediately, lights started coming on in Graham Hall. People were screaming and pouring outside. The dorm was brilliantly illuminated by the flames. Somebody must have pulled a fire alarm because suddenly faraway sirens filled the air. The city fire department was rushing to the fire on campus.

A little bit rattled, we watched the flames in awe. Then we heard crunches in the snow as someone ran toward us. The Nelson Hall arsonist ran by us carrying two empty gas cans. His black clothing was torn and smelled like a flooded carburetor. One leg of his slacks was smoldering. In the light of a streetlamp, we saw that one of his eyebrows was missing. He kept running, breathless and shouting as he went by, "I'm leaving, see you guys after Christmas."

Our pot of money was leaving also.

We moved through the darkness into the light and asked what happened. A fireman laughed, "Some fool tried to burn a snowball down." The Graham Hall boys eyed us warily.

Another fireman quipped, "Yeah, whatever idiot did it, just turned it into a solid block of ice!" The truth slowly dawned on us—by flaming the snowball, we had done something none of our research had taken into account. In the twenty-degree temperature, what had been a six-foot snowball was now a four-foot ice cube that wouldn't melt for another four weeks. The ice glistened in the flaming lights of the fire truck.

Lesser men might have been defeated. The next day, Ragar received an unexpected phone call—there was a new plan. The arsonist called from Haynesville, a town just across the Louisiana state line. He didn't like defeat. His grandfather had an old pickup truck he was going to borrow. His plan was to drive it through the snowball. We wanted to watch. He said the Snowball would break into small pieces that would melt quickly. He wanted thirty dollars for doing it. Anticipating the spectacle, we quickly collected the money.

A little before midnight, we were standing in the darkness. Soon, we heard the loud noise of a vehicle that seemed to have no muffler. Then we saw the old truck with a single headlight jump a ditch as it screamed across the campus toward the block of ice! We were excited just thinking about what was about to happen to that inanimate object that had become our nemesis.

When the battered old truck hit the snowball, pieces flew everywhere! Unfortunately, they were not pieces of the snowball but pieces of the truck. We heard extended moans from inside the wrecked truck. Soon the driver was crawling out of a window and running. But not soon enough. The guys from Graham Hall grabbed him and held him. One of them was shouting, "Somebody get some rope!"

Soon, rope appeared. The driver was stripped to his underwear. Five Graham Hall guys were pulling him atop the snowball and six others were staking his hands and feet down. Soon, he was secured to the icy snowball in the chilly night air. He, from our distance, seemed to be okay from the wreck, just cold from being strapped—practically naked—to the snowball-turned-ice-block.

We listened in the darkness to his screams for a while. We couldn't do anything because at least thirty Graham Hall boys surrounded the snowball.

Ragar spoke, "I'm tired. I believe I'll go to bed."

"Me too," Henson replied. Heads drooping, we all walked back across campus toward the jock dorm. It had not been our night.

The next day we found out the driver had no broken bones, just an assortment of bruises from the wreck. His grandfather's pickup would require a new radiator and some cosmetic work, projected to cost more than Ragar's friend was likely to earn from the coming summer's wages.

The last remnants of that ten-foot snowball were now just chunks of ice which would finally turn to water about a week later.

We had lost but it was a memorable effort.

The Aloha Lodge and Pancake House

AFTER GRADUATING FROM SOUTHERN ARKANSAS, I taught and coached high school for six glorious years—two in my beloved hometown, Hampton, and four at John L. McClellan High School in Little Rock. When I was coaching football in Little Rock, my brother, who would later become an eye doctor in Little Rock, was just starting his post-college life. It was 1968 and he was teaching biology in Hot Springs, Arkansas. He kept telling me about a Hot Springs guy he had become friends with; a young man who was planning on going to graduate school in England come fall. For now, he and Danny were meeting at The Aloha Lodge and Pancake House about three nights a week and discussing the day's events. Danny told me, "This guy is going to be president someday."

I replied, "Wait a minute, you meet a guy at a Pancake House late at night to eat and shoot the breeze—and you have now decided he is going to be president?"

"That's right."

I laughed, "Does this guy tell you that he is going to be

president?"

"No, we've never talked about it ... But I believe he will be." I laughed again.

Later that year, my brother introduced me to his buddy. He was an interesting guy, all right. The three of us all shared stories and had great conversations—none of it about political ambition.

Finally, Danny and I had to leave. As we were getting in the car, my brother questioned me, "Well, what do you think?" I took a moment to consider my answer.

Finally, I replied, "Someday the president of the U.S.A. will be Bill Clinton."

My brother smiled.

How I Ended Up in Film

1966. LITTLE ROCK. I LOVED COACHING AND TEACHING. I loved the coaches I coached with and the students I coached and taught. It was a good life. At the time, I thought I would never leave it. But after six years, the close-knit staff I loved was breaking up for other jobs and graduate schools. I was torn. I had always been a photographer and part-time artist interested in film. If I was ever going to pursue those interests, 1966 was the time to do it.

Pursue I did. I decided to go into the advertising business. The opportunity presented itself in a crazy way, but I was ready for a challenge. My first step was making ads to sell products on television—commercials. It all came to a head in the middle of track season. After practice each day, I would sketch storyboards for various imaginary products. The storyboard laid out, in graphic format, what a television commercial for a product might look like in a series of frames. If I were doing a commercial for television, the storyboard would be my visual shorthand for the concept, frame-by-frame. Almost daily, the other coaches offered comments on the work.

But I was stymied: how do you move from coaching high school track and football to producing commercials—or anything— that would actually be broadcast on television? I had no idea.

One early spring morning, I read in the Little Rock newspaper that the president of a national insurance agency, Frank Whitbeck, was planning to run for governor of Arkansas. Naively, I thought he should use me to do his political commercials. The article named his ad company, The Brandon Agency. My mental wheels began to turn. That night after track practice, I spent hours imagining the spots I would do for the client and sketching them out onto storyboards. I sketched panels on paper—each a step of the visual presentation.

On Thursdays, we had light, short workouts because of a track meet the next day. One Thursday, I slipped away and headed to downtown Little Rock to meet Jim Brandon, the head of The Brandon Agency, with whom I didn't have an appointment. In the car, I recited how I would tell him why a coach at a local high school should be the guy to direct and produce his candidate for governor's film media. I knew if I phoned for an appointment he would never see me.

Arriving at the office building near the downtown skyline, I stumbled through a conversation with the very pleasant receptionist. I was stumbling because it was at that moment I realized how ludicrous my pitch sounded. She looked at me, smiled, and— looking puzzled—said, "Okay, I'll go ask Mr. Brandon if he will see you."

I almost turned and fled.

The door to his office was partly ajar. I could barely hear the receptionist talking quietly to her boss. Hearing the refined tenor voice of Mr. Brandon was no trouble at all. "Why are you wasting my time with a ... a not even amateur!" Then, the door slammed all the way shut and only mumbled conversation reached me.

I was gathering the storyboards to ease out and spare the young woman having to tell me, "No way," when I heard her say, "Mr. Brandon will see you now."

Brandon's "why would I waste both our times talking about hiring a ..." was burning a hole through my brain as I entered his dark-paneled office, so I decided to address his fears directly.

The first thing I did was to answer Mr. Brandon's question. "Well sir, I'll shoot the spots and pay for them (so far so good) and if you don't like them, you don't have to pay" (not so good).

"Well, that's certainly an offer I don't often get. Let me see your storyboards."

I handed him the storyboards. He mused in silence for a while, then spoke, "I see you used some of the copy I had in my press release."

"Yes, sir ..."

"Well, they're not bad ... But this seems like madness."

"I understand, sir."

Mr. Brandon continued, "We do have weeks to go before the election. If I don't like them, I could replace them."

"Yes sir, you could. It will take me a couple of weeks to get a crew together ..."

He interrupted, "Son, you don't get it. We don't have that long in politics. Here's the deal. Even though it won't pan out, I will give you a chance at doing one of our spots because it is free. It is now Thursday, and you have the candidate for one day. Saturday. You can have him at eight in the morning. Oh, and I am crazy for doing this."

"Yes sir, thank you."

He looked at me over his horn-rim glasses with a little disdain, "Why do I do stuff like this? Call me with your location. Now leave."

I gathered the boards and walked through the outer office. The secretary smiled, "Good luck! He's not as cranky as he seems!" I smiled because I was elated.

By the time I hit the elevator, I was panicking. I had no camera, no crew, and no idea what I was going to do!

Returning to the school, I caught most of the coaches still in the gym facility offices.

I filled them in. They laughingly shook their heads and asked what I had talked myself into. Finally, Wayne Bass, one of the coaches, spoke up, "Okay, what can we do to help?"

"You're going to be my film crew—and maybe we can get a couple of our athletes to help."

Coach Charlie Payne asked, "Do you have a camera and lights?"

Before I could answer, Coach Glen Arnold (one of my first cousins), jumped in. "Maybe we can get the people who do our game films to loan us some equipment."

"A great idea!" Why hadn't it occurred to me? I called Ray-Chris Productions, the film processor that developed game film for about every football team in the state of Arkansas. I told them what was up. After they quit laughing, they told me to come down that night so they could loan me the needed gear. We arrived at the Ray-Chris studio late. Nonetheless, they were gracious and helpful. Most of their time was spent showing us how to load raw film into the camera. As it turns out, that was the most difficult part of the process. Five of us coaches struggled out of the production house at midnight carrying lights, sound gear, and cameras—feeling overwhelmed by the mission we had undertaken. We agreed to meet at my house on Friday night for a dry-run. We were trained football coaches, not film guys, and we had never filmed anything. In a heartbeat, we would be shooting spots for a gubernatorial candidate. How could we possibly go over everything before Saturday morning? I knew it was crazy. Still, with my fellow coaches at my side, I began to feel like we might have a chance ... Just a tiny chance.

I had talked to my Uncle J.L. Means, who was in the oil business. Knowing no one would ever hire me, he had said, "I tell you what, if you can talk them into hiring you, I will fund the costs of the spots."

In the early hours of Friday morning, I drove around the area until daybreak and found a horse ranch with beautiful white wooden fences and plenty of horses in the fields, a perfect location for the shoot. At noon on Friday, I returned to the ranch and negotiated with the owner for access and rights to film on his property. Nineteen hours after leaving The Brandon Agency, we had a location, equipment, and a small chance.

That night, after the track meet, the coaches and a couple of our athletes assembled at my house. Using some Polaroids I had shot of the location, we mapped out who would be doing what, where the best lighting would be, and what I would say to the candidate.

As the other coaches headed home to get some sleep, I went to Kmart. Thinking it would be impressive if everyone looked like a team, I bought matching shirts—beautiful, green silk-like t-shirts—and then added baseball caps that matched. I have to say, that after working for many years in the business, those coaches remain the best-looking film crew I ever worked with. Our "uniforms" shouted, "coordinated!" It at least looked like we knew what we were doing.

We were on set at 7 a.m. When the candidate, Mr. Whitbeck, stepped out of his long, black sedan, I introduced everyone. After he asked where we were based—"Dallas?"—I realized that he really didn't have a clue that he was looking at a bunch of coaches and jocks who were on a film set for the first time in their lives!

We set the camera up, I shouted "action," and everything rolled along, just as if we coaches were a real film crew. The candidate looked gubernatorial. At ease, he spoke in reassuring tones and followed our instructions. The coach behind the camera gave me a thumbs up sign when the picture in his viewfinder was convincing. The "sound coach" did the same when he believed the sound was coming through. By lunchtime, every shot on our list was "in the can." We all shook hands with the candidate. He told us what a professional group we were and waved goodbye.

As soon as he was out of sight, a collective cheer went up from our "production team," and we sprinted toward Ray-Chris where, like a dozen expectant fathers, we waited while our film was processed. An hour later, we waited on the output end of the processing machine to confirm the results. *We did actually record images, didn't we?*

Everyone was elated when the takes all looked and sounded like professional work. We had pulled it off! We called Jim Brandon and invited him to come by and look at the footage. He did so almost immediately. We watched Mr. Brandon as he watched our raw footage. His expression was motionless and he was silent. When it hit the end, he spoke, "Gentlemen, the footage looks very good." A weight lifted! Now we just needed to get him out of there so the Ray-Chris guys could explain how editing worked.

⁓

Watching commercials that we had created on more hope than know-how air during the primary race felt really good. We had delivered on our promise and surprised ourselves more than anyone else. Our efforts were rewarded on election night when our candidate won the party nomination.

Unfortunately, a tight race in the general election resulted in our man not becoming governor. Even so, nobody held our video productions at fault. The candidate sent us a complimentary note about the spots and Jim Brandon seemed pleased with himself, saying, "See, I am not as crazy as you think for hiring you."

Now you know how I ended up in the film business. However, that was just the beginning.

⌒

I want to skip forward by a few years to 1992. I had been invited to speak to the United States Chamber of Commerce. Over a thousand captains of industry packed a hotel ballroom—not for me—but to hear from a string of top corporate management executives and fast-rising Silicon Valley phenoms, the main participants in the event. I was just one of several small business speakers selected to tell, in my case, about how I got into the film business. I told it—to the apparent appreciation of the attendees. After the surprise applause settled down, I left the podium to find a place in the audience as the emcee introduced the next speaker. I was still trying to get settled into my seat when I heard my name called by the new speaker. I turned to see the elegant star of my first commercial, Frank Whitbeck, standing at the podium.

"Harry, that candidate was me and yours was a very interesting story!" The crowd responded laughing and applauding. It was one of those moments when it feels like everyone around you is hearing your daydream. "I never knew that my future was riding in the hands of a bunch of football coaches and their athletes." More laughter from the crowd. He stepped down, came to me and shook my hand, saying, "Good job." More applause.

It was a satisfying conclusion to the first chapter of my life in the media business. Smiling, I thought of how daring Jim Brandon had been.

Cabooses

MEANWHILE, BACK TO THE SEVENTIES ... Even though Jim Brandon, the president of the Brandon Agency, had trusted me to do the job for his political candidate, I was not sure he would use my little team of novice filmmakers (now made up of ex-students) again. For months, our Cinderella moment was little more than a chuckle-inducing memory. But on a cool, autumn day the phone rang, "Harry, Brandon here. I've got a client and I'm going to give you a shot."

An hour later, I stood on the plush carpeting in his office as he introduced me to two men from the railroad union. They explained that railroad management had an act on the ballot in the upcoming November election, an act that threatened to do away with cabooses. The crisis was cabooses, those red, cupola-capped railway cars that, for over a hundred years, were the last car on a train. Cabooses carried a couple of workers who oversaw the safety of the train. After all, it would be impossible for the engineer of a sixty-car train to look to the rear and spot anything wrong. The union believed it was foolish to eliminate this tradition that they considered a major bastion of railway safety. Management also wanted to eliminate a crew member from the main engine. The union felt that if you eliminated another crew member, you certainly could not maintain the vigilance you need to react to equipment failures (such as then-common *hot boxes*—basically overheated wheel bearings) or a hazard on the track.

I wanted this video production job badly. All my life, I had been a union man (and I always will be). Even though I am now mostly in management, I would not dream of producing a feature film or TV series without union blessings. I had belonged to the union when I spent my summers in high school and college, before football practice started, roofing large buildings—icons like Churchill Downs in Kentucky and the Indianapolis Speedway in Indiana.

The union men said, "Get back to us tomorrow on how you propose to design the spot, include your budget, and we will give you our decision."

With that, Jim escorted me to the door, where he whispered, "Listen, this has to be good. We have just enough money to produce one thirty-second spot and get minimal coverage statewide. The railroad owners have unlimited money and will probably air ten times as many spots as we can afford. Besides, we are eleven points behind in the polling right now."

Okay, I had figured out why he hired us. It was hopeless. The client had no money and we were the only ones desperate enough to take the job.

～

I didn't sleep well that night. By morning, though, I had a plan—for better or worse. I called my guys, Jim Roberson, Doug Jackson, Ron Roberson, Charlie Thurston, and Steve Beeson. I told them what I wanted to do, and asked them to put together a budget in an hour.

By noon, I called Jim Brandon to outline our plan. He said, "I'll call you back later." Click. I returned the phone to its cradle and turned to leave.

Before I reached the door, I was startled by the ringing phone. "Hello?"

"You're on. Start today." Click.

By afternoon, we had assembled an "all-American family" consisting of my two-year-old daughter, Stacy, bless her heart (she is an angel and she's suffered a lot for her dad over the years, by being in his commercials), her wonderful mother, Judy, and my insurance agent Mickey Wilson, who played the husband. We filmed them loading a picnic basket into their convertible (rented from Hertz) and driving away, wind in their hair and music playing. As soon as we finished the scene, we headed for a railroad crossing and set up in the middle of it with the camera pointed down the track. We were young and daring, it never occurred to us we needed to get Missouri Pacific's permission to be on their tracks. Or, maybe we knew that since they were our opponent in this election, there was not a snowball's chance in hell we could get permission.

Soon, we heard a train headed for us and we rolled the

cameras. It got closer and loomed in the viewfinder. The horn sounded as the engineer saw the guys and cameras on the track and got worried as he closed in at high speed—now less than a football field-length away. Finally, the train was twenty yards away, and I shouted, "Jump everybody, jump!" The train horn screamed as we rolled off the track! We turned back just in time to see the engineer leaning out the cab window with a hand signal meant for us.

Back in the editing bay that night we laid it out. We saw the smiling, happy family getting into the convertible and driving away. Lighthearted music swelled up. Soon, we saw a single frame of the train heading toward us in the distance. An ominous quick beep accompanied the train. As the spot moved along, louder beeps and more film of the train coming ominously closer. We saw the convertible approach an unmarked railroad crossing. One last frame of the train overwhelming the screen, whistle screaming. The sound of a huge crash. The screen went black. Silence. A beat. Then, over the black screen, we heard a baby crying. Yes, I talked my two-year-old daughter into crying, sorry Stacy. On the black screen, a legend appeared:

SAVE LIVES
VOTE AGAINST INITIATED ACT ONE.

In mid-October, the spot began its run on statewide television. The railroad corporations were still eleven points ahead.

A little after the ten o'clock news started, I got a call from a man I knew at the local NBC station. "Harry, our switchboard jammed right after the spot ran."

"What?"

"People are calling, threatening the railroad companies! Some wanted phone numbers and names at Missouri Pacific and Rock Island. One person even threatened to bomb Mo-Pac's headquarters in St. Louis!"

And so it continued. By midnight, Jim Brandon and the railroad union guys had called. They were getting supportive calls from everyone. We knew it affected the viewers—but would it change the polls? A week later we got the answer. The giant railroad companies had slipped to only a two-point lead. Union members were volunteering money to increase the number of times the spot could run.

That November election night, Initiated Act One went down in an inglorious defeat. Score one for the union working man!

The Man in the Window Seat

"I WASN'T SURE WHAT THE HELL TO DO, so I went to the railroad yard across the river in North Little Rock and jumped a freight headed east. I never looked back because I felt damn sure some jackass from the sheriff's office was hot behind me and I damned sure wasn't going to jail."

Okay, I should take this from the beginning.

January 27th, 1976. I was flying to Los Angeles from Little Rock to see if I could sell something to a major studio—or any studio for that matter. I arrived late at the American Airlines counter. The ticket agent hastily wrote as he spoke, "You fly with us a lot and we have one first class seat left to Dallas. I'm giving it to you. Sorry, you'll be in coach from Dallas." I thanked him profusely and hurried to the aircraft. Life was simple, no security check-in those days, just run and get on the plane.

In the first-class cabin, I saw the only vacant seat. As I approached, the very old man in the window seat glared at me. Obviously, he didn't want a seatmate. I sat down and said,

"Hello," to break the ice.

Nothing. The man, who was wearing a strange suit, glared at me and turned away. As the flight lifted off, he looked out the window. He said quietly, "That's how I left here last time."

I looked out to glimpse the railroad yard in North Little Rock. "Sir?"

He looked at me, "Son, what's your name?"

"Harry, sir."

He replied, "Where you headed?"

Dallas, sir."

"Stop the damn 'sir' stuff."

"Yes, sir ..." I caught myself.

His countenance finally softened, but only a little. Soon, he was asking me about my work. We kept conversing, talking about football, politics, and people. He told me he had met with Arkansas Governor, David Pryor, and that Pryor seemed like a good man.

～

The mystery gentleman and I landed in Dallas and made our way to the Los Angeles gate. I had to stop at a pay phone to call the office. I told him it was nice to meet him as he walked away nodding. I made the call, got on the plane, and headed to the coach section. As I moved through first class, he stopped me. "I explained to the stewardess that you were going to be sitting up here with me."

"Sir, I don't have the money to sit up here!" "Son, this damn airline does what I ask it to do. Sit the hell down."

"Yes, sir."

"It's a long way to Los Angeles and I don't want to have to make any new friends. It's not that you're that great." He smiled—I think.

It seemed that something about looking at that railroad yard as we left Little Rock made the tough old man in the strange suit want to talk about his life. It was apparent that I was the designated listener.

As we made our way to the West Coast, he told me what a tough childhood he had. "Poppa died when I was six years old and my mother had to take a bunch of jobs. By the time I was ten, I had hired myself out to a farmer, trying to help her. The farmer paid me two dollars a month and I thought I was making a damn fortune! When I turned sixteen, I decided it was time to leave. I didn't like the son-of-a-bitch that married my mother, so I forged enlistment papers and joined the damn Army."

"What happened?"

"They sent my ass to Cuba, where I was a mule wrangler. But it was over in three months, and I headed for Alabama. By the way, I did get an honorable discharge—some bastard New York newspaperman reported it was dishonorable. Had a lot of jobs in Alabama, including working on the railroad."

Railroads seem to have played a big part in his life.

He continued, "Got tired of what I was doing in Alabama, took a correspondence course in the law from LaSalle University, headed for Little Rock and started lawyering. I was damn good at it too!"

"What happened."

"I got a guy off on some debt he owed, and he refused to pay me. He was nasty about it, too. Even before we got out of the damn courtroom, he pushed me and called me a bastard or something like that."

"So you quit the law because of that?"

"No son, I quit the law because I have a bad temper and I beat the son-of-a-bitch half to death right there in front of the judge. So, I went home, got my stuff, headed to the freight yard, and got the hell out of town."

～

This is where we came in. For years after he left Arkansas, he failed at every "respectable" job until he ended up running a Shell gas station. To eke out a little better living, he started serving food. He suffered the drudgery for many years. He was facing living on his tiny Social Security check and was in his mid-sixties before he finally figured it all out. Didn't hurt that the governor of the state where he lived gave him an honorary title that he was able to incorporate into the name of his business—Colonel Sanders' Kentucky Fried Chicken.

We were at LAX and walking toward the exit where his limo driver awaited. He certainly attracted attention with his trademark white suit, black tie, white goatee, and handlebar mustache. "Boy, why is David Pryor, the governor of Arkansas, paid only ten thousand dollars a damn year?"

I actually knew the answer to that one but was not entirely sure I was correct. "I think it was it was set forth in the state

Constitution—1870-something—so it would take a constitutional amendment to change it. These days, I believe they make it up in expenses and stuff like that."

"Son, I hope so because I got chicken pluckers that make more than that." He laughed and disappeared into his limo. For me, other than meeting him, it would be a futile trip. I would have to wait a few more years to break into Hollywood.

My seatmate, Colonel Harlan David Sanders, Kentucky Fried Chicken's founder, died in 1980 at the age of ninety.

Back to the Caboose

LITTLE ROCK. 1972. Leroy Slaughter, our logistics manager at Centronics Productions (my small film company) buzzed me. "Jim Brandon on line one for you." I took the call.

"I have a job for you. It's just been two years, but the damn railroad companies are doing it again. They obtained enough signatures to get Initiated Act One on the November ballot again. Still trying to get rid of cabooses and good union people. Claim to their people that they are going to roll up the unions with twice as much money as they spent before. You want a job on the Titanic?"

"Jim, I always want a job."

"Okay, the unions have very little money, so again we can only afford to make one spot. Going to be hard to top your last one."

"We'll figure out something."

We talked to the unions, did our research, and made a decision on the commercial we wanted to create. We needed a simple spot and one with an actor and not the actual person it portrayed, which we felt would be too graphic. We ran it by the unions and The Brandon Agency. They blessed it and we went to work.

There have always been good actors who call Little Rock home but of course they then had to have other jobs to support themselves. We picked a great actor who worked at a jewelry shop. He was now a railroad man!

～

We decided to do it late at night on the same piece of track we shot on two years ago. We didn't know we had picked Missouri Pacific's track, but we would later.

The weather cooperated. It was an unusual night in October. As if on cue, a light fog descended upon the area. We set up multiple cameras and splashed just the right amount of light on our actor. In our commercial, the man supposedly had one leg, so we carefully tied up the actor's leg behind him. From the front angles, he truly looked as if he were missing a limb.

The fog, the darkness, the actor, the sense of foreboding— everything was perfect.

I shouted, "Roll cameras," and we were off. The "one-legged" actor, on crutches, hobbled up onto to the railroad track. The fog coated the scene with just the right amount of hopelessness. He spoke.

"I worked on a train crew in Missouri. It was two years ago, and they had passed a law like Initiated Act One. It was an icy December night and because of the new law we were short-handed. I was pulling duty for what before would have been two men ..." He started to cry, then continued, "Tired, I was climbing a rail-car ladder when I slipped and fell under the steel wheels." By now, the tears were flowing down his face. "Please vote against Initiated Act One." He continued to stand on his crutches, his cheeks glistening. As if heaven-sent, somewhere, far away in the foggy darkness, a lonely train whistle cut thru the night. We knew we had just seen a great performance by a great artist.

⁓

What happened next brought us back to reality quickly.

Click. The unmistakable sound of a cartridge being pumped into a rifle. Looking toward the woods, we saw three men emerging from the dark with weapons pointed toward us. I quickly glanced back toward the track to see our actor take his leg down and sprint into the dark woods.

"Well, well, looks like we caught some criminals trespassing on our track. Why don't the rest of you run?" Addressing me, he added, "We will just shoot you and have it over with." He was a large, menacing guy. Nobody moved. A car with a long antenna on the back and flashing yellow lights pulled up from an access road onto the side of the track. Missouri Pacific Security was painted on the driver's door. The lead guy demanded, "Who's in charge here?" The crew hesitated, but they all were looking at me. The guy turned and pointed the rifle at me, "You sonofabitch! You almost cost me my job two years ago by filming on our property with that little baby thing. Get in the middle of the track and sit down!" Seeing no merit in argument, I sat on the track. His goons quickly encircled me and handcuffed my hands behind my back.

I noticed that my crew had slowly backed off the railroad right of way and that the film magazine with the primary footage had been removed from the camera and placed under a jacket near our van.

The guy dared me to get up and run so he could shoot me. "No, I'm comfortable sitting here. I'm sure the police will hear about this and will be here in a little while."

"Good, 'cause I caught you trespassing."

I mustered the bravado to speak again, "Yes, sir. I'm sure the union will want to hold a press conference tomorrow and expose how you threatened to kill us over the election."

Addressing his goons, the leader finally spoke, "Watch this guy and club him if he tries to escape." He looked at my crew, "Same for these guys. Don't let them leave. Let me get St. Louis on the radio." With that, he seated himself in the car, the yellow flashers still strobing the scene and the sixteen-foot antenna standing sentinel. Soon, I could hear muffled voices over the radio. My crew, as usual, thought the situation was funny.

Soon, the guy got out of the car and came toward me, "Okay, St. Louis says we can let you go but to warn all of you that the next time you get caught filming on our track will be the last mistake you ever make." His deputies unlocked the handcuffs and I got up and walked to the van. We all piled in, stone-faced, and drove away.

After a mile or so, everybody erupted in laughter until tears were streaming. I asked,"Guys, what the hell are you laughing at? He was threatening to kill me!"

"No, we are laughing because we have never seen anybody run as fast as our 'one-legged' actor! He's somewhere in these woods!"

Paul Fisk the staff writer interjected, "We can't go back and look for him because they don't know we got a take, and they will be waiting to make sure we don't come back."

We started putting in calls to the actor's home. Just before daybreak, he returned our frantic calls to let us know he had made it home. He was scratched up and bruised from his romp through the woods, but okay. We all congratulated him on his performance.

∽

We edited the spot and delivered it to the agency. I called Jim Brandon and explained all that had happened. I finished with, "Mr. Brandon, you know the spot is good, but the railroad detectives saw the actor run into the woods. They might cause us some trouble."

"Why would they? I have already seen their spots and they are using actors, too."

"Okay, but I just wanted to alert you."

Later in the day, he called. "I have seen the spot and so have the unions. It's fantastic! We are overjoyed and can't wait to get it on the air!" "

October arrived and the railroad companies' Act One pulled ahead in the polls because they had spent tons of money. Our pro-union spot started and, like two years before, it riled the public. Immediately, the polling on Act One showed its support starting to decline rapidly. The union and the agency were very satisfied clients.

The days of October ground by with worries of the union's limited airtime budget, yet polling steadily turned in the union's favor.

On Friday before the Tuesday election, I was sitting in my office when the phone rang. It was our actor. He was whispering and sounding terrified, "Harry, the shop is filled with news cameras and reporters. They know it was me in the spot and they want to interview me! What should I do?"

Not thinking very clearly, I replied, "Well, I would try to avoid them!" I should have told him to say, "Yes it was me, and the other side used actors also." I just wasn't that quick on my feet. I alerted everyone and said there was trouble. I have to admit, the railroad moguls were smart to hold off unveiling something like this till the weekend before the election. By holding this revelation until then, they left us no response time.

I got home and watched as the local news, which had just started. The story about the union using an actor in the spot led on all local news reports. Everybody was guessing at the outcome, which was then too soon to influence. Sure enough, the last-minute revelation had affected voter sentiment. The Act One vote was moving up. Our fears were confirmed late on Friday night when spot-polling showed our side behind again.

I called the union representative, "You, of course, know we all decided not to use the real victim because it might hurt his chance of a lawsuit and might be too much for the viewers ... But now, if he will, we have to film him."

The rep pondered it for a moment. "Okay, we'll give it our best shot. I am going to call my people and have them meet me at his house outside of Aurora, Missouri. I'll drive all night and see what we can do."

I talked to my guys. We met at the office, packed equipment at the crack of dawn on Saturday, and headed to Central Flying Service, boarding a chartered plane to Missouri. On arrival, we drove into the country to the victim's house. The lawn was crowded because railroad management had sent a team down from St. Louis. Their message: if the victim decided to help the union, management would pull the settlement they had offered.

Our union guy came out of the house and said we were stalemated. The victim we wanted to film was torn between doing the right thing and receiving money his family needed. As he was speaking, more union guys who knew the victim and had worked with him arrived and walked directly into the house. Our union contact commented, "Those guys are the ones he worked with. If they can't get him to do it, we are finished."

An hour passed.

Another half hour passed.

A little later, the sound of a song drifted from the inside of the house—just fragments at first. The singing got louder. The guys inside were singing an old folk song, *If I Die a Railroad Man.* Jim Roberson, my cinematographer spoke, "Guys, I believe we are going in—get the equipment!" We were indeed going in. To do so, we had to run a gauntlet of disgruntled railroad managers and attorneys still menacingly crowded onto the lawn.

Inside, we set up to film our person of interest, a gentle soul with a sense of humor. We were right not to have used him—it would have been cruel. Both his legs were missing right at the crotch. He had to be propped up on the bed with pillows on each side to keep him from falling over. Jim started the camera. It was all I could do to ask the injured man to tell his story. He never cried but everyone else in the room did as he told his personal, powerful story.

Midway through the story, a pillow slipped from his side and—with his arms still in casts after several months—he had no way to stop himself from falling. Slowly, he began to tip to the side, like a bowling pin in a slow-motion tumble. Jim looked at me in a panic and I shook my head. We were not going to stop his rotation. He never changed tone or quit talking until his head landed on the mattress. Finally, he finished, "And that is what happened."

We cut the camera, and everyone rushed in to set him upright using the pillows on the bed. Continuing his incredible good-naturedness, he stopped laughing only long enough to say, "Harry, if you had cut that camera, I was going to shoot you!"

That's what I thought! The guilt faded away!

∿

We flew back to Little Rock and processed the film. It was just as good as we thought. The Brandon Agency called a 10 a.m. press conference for Sunday morning at a Holiday Inn on Broadway—between the state Capitol and the banking skyscrapers.

The place was full of cameras and reporters from the Arkansas press. We had a projector in place with the film clip loaded and ready. I walked in with my crew and headed straight to the microphone. "We just wanted to show you why we did not want to exploit the actual victim. We will show you this film, but we will not make it available for you to air. Roll the film, please."

Our producer Doug Jackson hit the switch, and the projector whirred. Everyone was horrified by the extent of the injuries and also captivated by the victim's grace. The experience reminded me of a 1940s movie. As soon as the film ended, there was bedlam as reporters shouted questions and dashed from the room to the small bank of pay phones in the lobby.

I must admit, it did feel like redemption. Jim Brandon thanked us for the effort and said we had fought a Goliath and done the best we could. We had.

The story blanketed the TV news that Sunday night. We were told spot check polls showed that public sentiment was moving back toward our union guys, but Tuesday was upon us and we had too far to go. I wish we could report a good ending but, alas, we lost by a tiny margin. Not long after, as they eventually did in every state, the little red cabooses disappeared from the rails. Forever.

⌒

Several of those film crew members on that small project decades ago (almost all former students of mine), left the film business and became successful by founding companies in other areas, including Charlie Thuston in construction and Ron Roberson in finance.

Four of them remained in the industry with me, as I made my way toward Hollywood. Doug Jackson, known as one of the best producers in Hollywood—and the best friend one can have—produced with his partner, Tommy Thompson, a legend in Hollywood, all of our shows until our beloved Tommy was taken from us far too soon. Since then, Doug has continued to produce our shows alone.

Jim Roberson, our brilliant cinematographer, serves on our shows (as well as others) as director of photography and is treasured in the industry for his artistic skill and loyalty.

Doug and Jim are with us on every project we do.

Sadly, Paul Fisk and LeRoy Slaughter both went home early. But we don't abandon our fellow warriors, and we will always consider them, plus Tommy, as part of every project we do. We miss them all.

Has Hollywood Called?

OCTOBER 1977. IT WAS A LATE-AUTUMN NIGHT AND I COULDN'T SLEEP for the usual reasons. The TV commercial business was in a terrible slump, and I was hurting financially. My little company was down to almost nothing. I spotted a *Reader's Digest* magazine and causally picked it up. Thumbing through it, I came upon an interesting-looking story. "John Baker's Last Run" was the true story about an Olympic runner. When doctors told John Baker he had cancer, he decided to devote what little time he had left on earth to coaching a rag-tag band of little girls who had formed an AAU track team in New Mexico. Long before I reached the end, I felt tears streaming down my face. The ending, the team winning a national championship in St. Louis on the very day John died in New Mexico, finished me off.

I watched the *Johnny Carson Show* but kept thinking about what a human-spirit-triumphs-in-the-end movie John Baker's story would make. Then I pushed those thoughts from my mind thinking that surely, if it was in the magazine, some enterprising producer had already secured the film rights and had a team scheduled to shoot it. Plus, I wouldn't know how to start making contact with the subjects because the article didn't even say where the team was based in New Mexico.

Sometime after midnight, I decided to take a shot anyway—a choice that started in motion a series of events that would change my life.

∽

At my wits end about where to begin my search for the team, I dialed the number for the New Mexico State Police Headquarters in Albuquerque. After four rings, I was about to hang up. Then, "New Mexico State Police."

"Sir, this is going to sound crazy, but I am looking for someone ..." I explained the story I had read. With a hangdog tone, I admitted that I was sure he couldn't help but maybe he could point me in the right direction.

After a pause, he spoke again, "I loved that guy ... Went to high school with him. Nice family, his father runs the convention center here in town. Got a pencil?"

I scrambled to find one, "Yeah, I've got one."

He gave me the home number of the Baker family and said good night.

I finally went to bed knowing I would get up the next morning to find out from the family that someone had already bought the rights.

The next day, I nervously called the family's home number. A woman answered. "Hello, Mrs. Baker?"

"Yes, this is Polly Baker. Who is this?"

I blurted out the whole thing, how I loved her son's story, and how I would like to find a way to do it as a movie. Then, either to let her—or myself—down gently, I conceded my assumption that some other production company was already signed up.

"No they're not. Several companies have called but we haven't felt liked discussing it."

"Well, when you get ready. I wish I could be considered."

"You will be." That sounded good.

The conversation kept going. She quizzed me about my life, where I went to college, family and other things. She then told me she knew Little Rock well.

I asked how.

She told me a story about her husband's earlier days in the entertainment business. Then she surprised me by revealing that, in the late 1940s, her husband, a comic, had toured with the famous comedian, Danny Thomas. They had toured the nation. The Bakers' were getting tired of the road, and when the tour hit Little Rock, they made a decision to change their lives. They quit show business. Deciding to stay in Arkansas, the Bakers enrolled at Henderson State Teacher's College in the small town of Arkadelphia, about seventy miles south of Little Rock.

I was shocked. "Really! My mother went to college at Henderson for a while there!"

She laughed and replied, "Who knows, I might have known her." We talked a while longer. After beseeching her to keep me in mind, I gave her my phone numbers and bid her good day.

At least, she had left me with the impression that I would be considered.

That night, I was at the office late and was startled when the phone rang. It was Polly Baker. She said, "My husband is also on the line." She introduced us, and then said, "I was telling him about you, and we have decided we want you to have the rights to our son's story."

Stunned, I was a moment recovering my voice. Somehow, I managed to keep from squeaking as I replied, "I cannot tell you how much I appreciate this!"

"We know you will do the right thing with his story."

I wanted to do right, but as the months dragged on and I could not even convince a single soul to listen to my pitch, I grew increasingly disheartened.

John Baker's mother was wonderful. I would call her and tell her how slow it was going, and *she would cheer me up!* Her grace and patience were nothing short of remarkable.

October rolled around again. On a rainy Friday afternoon, I was in the office alone with nothing to do. The phone, which probably had not rung in several days, jarred me. "Hello?"

On the other end, I heard a person say she was with Brut Productions, a company that was soon to merge with Columbia Pictures. "We heard you had the rights to *John Baker's Last Run.* Is that so?"

"Yes, I have the option on it. Why?"

"We are interested and wonder if you would have some time to talk to our development people on Monday about selling it to us."

"No, I have had it this long and I told his mother I would make sure it is done right, so I can't sell it to you—but I will surely talk to see what kind of deal we might make."

"Excuse me, I need to ask someone a question." Click. An agonizing wait followed but then she came back on line. "Well, they don't think it will work, but they will listen to you on Monday."

I was excited. After a year of nothing, someone wanted to talk! I pulled the story back out and began to re-read it. The phone rang again. Alas, probably Brut saying they don't want to talk. "Hello?"

"Yes, this is Danielle from Universal Television. We hear you have the rights to the John Baker story."

I said yes and to let me get back to them at the first of the week. She pushed to talk right away, but I stalled her until Monday. Fifteen minutes later, the phone rang and it was Warner Bros. TV on the line. By then, I was getting good at pushing everyone a week!

This was exciting! Then the phone rang one more time. This time, it was a law firm in Los Angeles on the line. They wanted their client, Donny Osmond, to play the lead role in the movie and they had already talked to a network that was interested. I thought he was too young for the role and didn't know if he could act. However, since I liked the firm representing him, I assured them that we would talk.

It was an amazing day. I had put them all off until the next week so I could try to think clearly about which direction to go. By Sunday, I felt I had to go to Los Angeles and talk with each company in person in order to get what I wanted out of the deal. What I wanted was a chance to work on the picture as the actual producer. Since I had no presence in Hollywood at that time, I knew I was facing an uphill challenge.

My plan to eyeball each potential partner was all well and good ... There was one large problem. I had no money to buy a plane ticket to Los Angeles. I was in huge debt to Worthen Bank and Trust in Little Rock for loans that had kept me going this far. I knew it would be difficult to get another loan to finance my trip. My only hope was the young Worthen banker, Randy Reagan, one of the smartest guys I had ever met. He would be for it but the guys above him wanted him to quit dealing with *dreamers*—people whose ideas weren't conventional mainstream business plans.

Monday mornings were when all we dreamers usually went to Randy for more money to chase dreams—and this Monday was no different. When I arrived at the Worthen Bank Tower, two of the other usual dreamers were already seated in the waiting room ahead of me. We each apprehensively awaited our chance to plead for Randy's help. When it was my turn—last—I told Randy what was going on, that I just needed short-term help to pay some overdue bills and fly to Los Angeles for a few days to make a deal.

"I don't know, my bosses want me to cut you off. I am under a lot of pressure." A brief silence followed ... Then he sighed, "Okay ... Wait here and let me go upstairs and talk to someone."

It was a long half-hour before he came back to his desk. "All right, here is the deal. After me pleading your case forever, they have agreed to let me loan you an additional $7,500. Here's the catch, they said if you don't come back with a signed deal and check, it's over. They'll sue you and they will probably fire me!"

"Randy, thank you!"

He laughingly waved me off, "Just go get a deal. Save my job."

～

Monday afternoon, I called and talked to my new friends in the West and said I wanted to come out and talk in person. To my relief they all agreed. I was headed to Hollywood!

I was on a flight Tuesday to Los Angeles. I had cash but no credit card that wasn't maxed to the limit. The first thing I did when I got off the plane and outside the terminal was ask a baggage man if he had any idea where I could rent a car without a credit card.

He laughed, "Man, that's a tough one. I think you might can go a few blocks over on Sepulveda to a place called Ace Cars and do it." I thanked him, jumped in a cab and headed to Ace.

Arriving at the address, obviously a former gas station, I saw no cars out front. I went inside the rundown looking building, anyway. In what had once been the cashier's room of the gas station, I found four guys sitting around a folding card table, playing poker. They ignored me for several minutes while they finished the hand they were playing. Speaking of hands, I noticed one of them was missing two fingers on his left hand. Between that and the Brooklyn accents that dominated the room, it did make an Arkansas boy wonder. None of them was wearing anything approaching business attire.

One of the tougher ones, named Artie, spoke, "Yeah?"

"I was told you might have cars to rent to a traveler who has no credit card."

"Maybe, you got any damn cash?"

"I do."

"Then we got a car. Milo, bring the Pinto around." He then turned back to me. "Now come over here and let's get this done. Twenty-five dollars a day, you buy the gas, and don't put over fifty miles a day on the car. Oh, plus you pay in full up front."

Moments later, a beat up, red Ford Pinto came into view. I saw the reason for the fifty miles a day—the red Pinto might not have made it further than that.

"Do I need to fill out any paperwork?"

"No, just give me your driver's license and let me copy the number." I hand him the card. "Arkansas! You a long way from home, kid! What the hell are you doing out here?"

I proceeded to explain in probably a little too much detail. Artie asked, "Kid, you don't have a credit card, but you do have a plane ticket, right?"

"Yes, I do."

"Then give it to me and you can get it when you bring the car back. If you don't bring the car back, we'll come looking for you. Got it?"

"Yes, sir, I get it."

I squeezed into the beat-up Pinto and headed for my first

appointment, the law firm representing Donny Osmond. We assembled in a conference room, where several attorneys sat around a long conference table listening to me discuss the project. I will never forget how nice they were—even when I told them that I didn't think their client was right for the part. We kept talking and I revealed more and more about how things were tough, and I couldn't make a mistake.

Finally, one of the older attorneys said he understood. He said he had read the story and he didn't think Donny would work for the part. He said that the last thing he wanted to allow was for Donny to do something that would hurt his career. He kept speaking, "I know you are at a tough position in your career and I know how hard it is to break through out here. Moreover, I need to tell you that you're in trouble. You can't meet with studios and deal with their people without good people of your own. We'll forget about Donny doing the deal, but you need representation. We are going to loan you a lawyer."

"Sir?"

He continued, "We don't take on small clients like you, but I am going to see if one of our attorneys will go with you to all your meetings to make sure you are not taken advantage of."

"Sir, I don't know what to say!"

"Say nothing. I just can't let you get slaughtered on your first deal—bad for Hollywood's reputation."

They found someone who would go on this ride with me and only charged the minimum five percent of whatever the deal was that lawyers in Hollywood charge long-time clients for making a deal—no premiums. By the way, my new lawyer who just loved adventure and considered accompanying me a crazy adventure, was Joe Horacek, who also represented Barbara Streisand and Michael Douglas, among other major stars. This guy driving a beat-up red Pinto around Los Angeles was more than a little stunned!

Joe Horacek was one of the most likable attorneys I had ever met. I believe he worked just as hard for me as he worked for his famous clients.

We talked to everyone and chose to go with Columbia Pictures Television—now Sony Television. We agreed to meet them at the studio on Friday at noon to close the deal. It turned out to be a rainy day with even a few claps of thunder, something that almost never happens in Los Angeles. I remarked to Joe that I hoped this wasn't a sign.

Soon, we were seated in a conference room at Columbia as two lawyers walked in, one carrying a folder. They knew Joe and greeted him warmly (but I could tell they were a little perplexed as to why he was representing me). Then, they introduced themselves to me. "Harry, we know the studio really wants to do this deal and we are all so excited you are here! I have the deal letter for you to look over and sign and we can wrap this thing up."

He placed the deal letter in front of me and I started reading. The letter said I would be named as the producer of the show and would get the amount of money we had agreed upon. I read it through carefully again. "Here is what bothers me, it says I will be 'named producer of the show.' What I want to do is actually produce the show, not just have the name."

They acted as if they were stunned. "Harry, you have no experience out here. You're from Arkansas—we don't know what things you produced there. The studio would just never let this happen. There's too much at risk here. Just take the money, we'll put your name on the film and you can take a vacation to the Bahamas, come out for the premiere and your name will be listed as the producer. It's good, really good."

The disappointment rolled across me like a steamroller. I hesitated a moment, why not just take the money, give it up? Forcing my feelings down didn't work, and I replied, "No, I will not sign the letter if it just gives me an honorary title. I want to actually produce the show."

The Columbia lawyer said, "Harry, I can tell you that is not going to happen."

Joe, interceded, "Guys, just go talk to your people and see what you can do."

They disappeared and Joe turned to me, "If they say 'no' when they come back, what do you want to do? None of the other deals even approaches this one."

"You know I'm starving but I can't care about the money. If I am not really doing it, I might as well give it up because it ends my career in this business anyway."

"Okay, I'm with you." Outside, the rain was coming down ever harder. A big clap of thunder shook the floor-to-ceiling plate glass windows of the conference room.

The Columbia duo returned. "Sorry, they won't do it."

That hurt.

∼

Joe stood, "Well, we have many good offers and we are out of here. Let's go Harry." He dragged me from the chair, and we started down the long second-floor hallway toward the stairs. Joe said, "They are bluffing. They will catch us by the time we get to the stairs."

The storm continued outside. We reached the stairs and started down "I am sorry, I would have bet they would have called us back." We continued to the glass lobby and outside into what had become a pretty bad rainstorm. We crossed the street and Joe unlocked his car. Soaking from the downpour, we stepped into his Mercedes. Just as we reached to pull our doors closed, among the lightning and thunder, we heard a noise.

We looked back toward the building where the studio attorneys were holding the doors open, motioning us back in with their hands, and shouting above the thunder and rain, "Come on back in. Let's keep working on it!" Now soaked to the skin, Joe and I crossed the street and headed back into the building.

Soon, a new letter was drafted, giving me what I wanted. I was named the active producer of the film. Yes, there would be executive producers, etc., but I would be in charge of the actual production, just what I wanted. I forced myself to read the letter again—carefully.

"Are you happy, now?"

They appeared startled when I said, "There is just one more thing."

"What the hell is it? You got everything you asked for?" Joe's eyes showed his amazement, also. He was clearly puzzled, perhaps even shocked.

"See this, where it says I will receive a check for $25,000 when the deal is signed?"

"Yes, what about it?"

"It's signed, I want the check." This sent them over the edge.

"Harry, look, it always says that, but you have to know it takes a couple of weeks to get the check written. We will mail it to you as soon as it comes."

The other attorney jumped in, "Listen, you know that Columbia Pictures is owned by Coca Cola, so all checks are approved and sent out from our New York office."

"I told my bank I would come back with a check."

"Well we can't do that."

I don't know why but it escaped my mouth, "Then let's go, Joe." We rose to leave.

"Wait, let us take a try at it." The Columbia guys left. Joe looked at me sideways, smiled, and shook his head.

Another forty-five minutes ticked by before they walked back into the room, one holding up something that looked like a check. I recognized it as a *counter check*. It was something banks used to allow, a blank check without even the account holder's number printed on it. You had to fill in your account number also.

"You see this?"

"Yes, it's a counter check."

"Right, and according to the comptroller's staff, it is the first counter check Coca-Cola has issued since the 1920's."

They handed it to me. Slowly, carefully, my eyes scanned every detail. It read $25,000 for the first phase. I smiled and said, "Thank you."

They kiddingly replied, "Now, get the hell out!"

Late that Friday afternoon, the rain had quit and the sun was bright. I was grateful for that, since the windshield wipers on the Pinto didn't work. I rolled into Ace Cars about five o'clock. When I walked in, the poker game was going on. Nobody got up from the table. Artie shouted, "Harry! We didn't have to come looking for you! How'd it go?"

When I told them, they seem genuinely excited about my good fortune. "Damn, that is so great!" While Artie was giving me my airline ticket back, they asked all sorts of questions about my deal and when they could expect to watch the TV movie on CBS. Actually, I decided I liked these guys and their Brooklyn accents. That is how I ended up driving a banged-up red Pinto around L.A. for the first several months, as I commuted back and forth from Little Rock to Los Angeles. I would go into Ace and they would always be playing cards. Seeing me, they would get excited and shout, "Hey, our buddy from Arkansas is here, bring out the Pinto!" They were as excited as I was when things progressed. I never saw another car there that seemed like it was for rent and I never figured out what these guys really did at Ace Cars. I always figured I should not ask and leave well enough alone.

I was partnered with two of the best, smartest, and most

successful executive producers you could ever hope to do your first project with—Jim Green and the late Alan Epstein. They immediately became my friends for life. Their company had an overall deal with Columbia Television and I had a deal to produce a film, if we could sell it. They would be my guides through this new adventure.

To make a film you first had to get some network to buy it. At that time, there were only about four places (and HBO was just getting underway) you could do that. The first long weeks were spent talking to all the networks and narrowing down who might want to do the picture. Our hope was CBS, since they did the most prestigious and highest-budgeted movies in the television industry.

The call we wanted finally came—CBS was interested! The head of the movie division, Robert Wunsch, wanted us to come over and talk about it. We were in his office later that afternoon. Smart, sophisticated and well-versed in all the arts, he wanted to know how we were going to approach the film. He wanted to greenlight it, but felt it was special and wanted to give it the justice he felt it deserved.

We had been talking about writers for some time and could not come up with anybody that he felt could do the project justice. This guy was tough. This was clearly going downhill. I didn't say much, just listened and became more and more anxious because I didn't know enough to contribute to the conversation.

As we lost even more ground it appeared the meeting was about to be cut short, I grew desperate. Finally, like I was in a first-grade classroom, I raised my hand. Everybody looked at me and stopped talking. Wunsch, after a long beat, said, "Yes?"

Sort of embarrassed, I replied, "I have a person in Arkansas, who I think could do this script. His name is..."

Alan Epstein, quickly grabs my arm, squeezes it (as in *be quiet*) and interrupted, "Harry, Bob doesn't have the time to hear about writers from Arkansas."

Wunsch jumps in, "No, no. Let him finish. What writer did you have in mind, Harry?"

I continue, "A good friend of mine named Bill Harrison."

Wunsch reacted, and the room became quiet. Allen gave me a look and started to speak but Bob Wunsch interrupted, "Harry, you wouldn't happen to be talking about Dr. William Harrison, would you?"

"Yes sir."

"How good of a friend is he?"

"Good enough to help me out when I need it."

Another long beat. Wunch carefully chose his words ..."Harry, if you can get the famed novelist and author of the *Rollerball* novel, plus screenplay for the Norman Jewison/Jimmy Caan film, committed to this project, then this is a done deal."

We were all stunned for a second. Finally, I said, "Sir, can you tell me where I can go and phone him?" He pointed to an empty office. I entered the office and shut the door, wondering if my career had just started or just ended.

We had a theater screening several weeks before the film appeared on CBS Television. The theater was filled to capacity.

No empty seats, certainly not the ones I had reserved for the guys from Ace Cars.

The film starred Timothy Bottoms, Ed Begley, Jr, Rip Torn and Allyn Ann McLerie and was directed by Stuart Margolin. It won several awards including the prestigious Christopher Award. It was a great project to work on and led me to a multi-year deal with Columbia Television.

Thank you, Bill Harrison. I owe it all to you and miss you, my friend.

~

I mentioned earlier in this chapter that in those days there were always a couple of other dreamers that, on numerous Monday mornings, were in Randy Reagan's second floor waiting area. One of them was Wayland Holyfield—he worked in an ad agency that I did some commercials for. He didn't want to be there, he wanted to be in Nashville doing what he dreamed of— writing songs. He finally worked things out and headed East. Did it work out? I think so! He, so far, has written forty Top Ten hits and fourteen number one hits! Some of his best-known songs are *Could I Have This Dance, Some Broken Hearts Never Mend, Till The Rivers All Run Dry, You're the Best Break This Old Heart Ever Had, Only Here For a Little While, Meanwhile,* and *Nobody Likes Sad Songs.*

The other person was Fred. He had a new idea for moving packages around the country but nobody at the bank other than Randy Reagan thought it was a good idea. They said none of it made sense. Randy was stopped from making further loans, leaving Fred no way out. Finally, on the last Friday his fledgling company could survive, he withdrew the remaining sixty-six hundred dollars he had in the bank and went to a place he had never been—Las Vegas. And he did something he had never done—he played blackjack!

When the Saturday sun dawned in Las Vegas, Fred had won over eighteen thousand dollars.

Fred headed back to Little Rock to pay his employees. On the next Wednesday, Fred reached a deal with General Dynamics— persuading them to put over twenty million dollars into his business nobody thought was a good idea.

⌒

You're probably wondering what the name of Fred Smith's struggling little business was. You've probably heard of it. It was called Federal Express.

The Blue and the Gray
and a Man Named Sam

I DON'T WANT TO PACK THIS BOOK WITH TALES OF HOLLYWOOD—that book should stand on its own (and will come later, if I get around to it). However, I did want to mention one more small story. After I did several movies at Columbia, the studio offered me a producer's contract—one that allowed me to continue to live in Little Rock and gave me one round-trip plane ticket per week between Little Rock and Los Angeles. I gladly accepted.

Early in my tenure, Columbia Vice President of Production Seymour Friedman, a legendary studio tough guy, born in the U.S. and schooled in England, called me in on a Monday morning. He informed me I was going to be one of two producers on a very high profile eight-hour miniseries, *The Blue and the Gray*, the most expensive television mini-series they had done to date. Since I was a former history teacher, he thought I would be a good fit to co-produce the project. He continued, "Talk to Hugh Benson (the other appointed producer) and get location scouting underway by tomorrow. We're behind already!"

By the next afternoon, Hugh and I—plus our location scouts and production manager—were in the air headed to the state of Washington to see if maybe it had enough of the scenery we needed to do the entire series there. It didn't. We next headed to the Napa Valley region of California and found they also had very few of the things on our checklist. By Friday, we were in the eastern U.S., looking at perhaps shooting near actual Civil War battlegrounds. We quickly found the areas around them all over-developed. We also found officials in those areas less than excited about the prospect of a large film production in the midst of their crowded park areas. Any of the locations we scouted would have required moving the entire filming operation several times and probably to several states to access the many kinds of scenes the series would require. We took all this information in, knowing company relocations are very expensive in the film business.

⌒

Discouraged, I flew from the East Coast to Little Rock late Friday night and worried about finding a location to do this gigantic, twenty-eight week movie shoot.

On Saturday morning I was immersed in site search home-work. On Monday morning, I flew back to Los Angeles and headed straight for Seymour's office. He spoke first, "I hear the location scout didn't go well."

"Yes sir, but I believe I have found a place we can shoot it all and *never* have to change locations."

The word "never" caught his attention. He paused and looked at me for a beat, "Where would that be?"

"North Arkansas, near Fayetteville and Fort Smith." He replied in a proper British accent, "I don't know how to get to Arkansas, never heard of those towns and this company has never shot anything in that state."

For a half hour, I laid photos in front of him of period homes, period buildings, a couple of U.S. Park Service-controlled—but uncrowded—Civil War battle sites and main streets of towns that could work as Civil War era. He studied them ... and studied them. Finally, he spoke, "Okay, shoot it there. Now get out, I've got a meeting."

"Thank you, sir. I'll go tell Hugh."

I walked out of his office and closed the door, but it soon opened again and he called to me, "Harry!"

I turned around, "Yes sir?"

"One other thing. If this goes wrong, you will never work in this town again." No, he didn't smile, he turned and closed the door. I stood there a moment, sighed, and walked to Hugh's office.

Shooting went very well in Northwest Arkansas, so well that some of the actors and crew even bought land around the Fayetteville area. The consensus was it was the best, most problem-free shoot any of the crew members had ever worked on. Co-operation by the communities—led by my friend and owner of the oldest bank in Fayetteville, Hayden McIlroy—made our jobs remarkably stress-free. Every response from the state, captained by Film

Commissioner Joe Glass, was perfect. Van Buren, Prairie Grove and all of the other small towns in the area made our crews feel welcome and respected.

Seymour flew to Fayetteville about six weeks into the shoot. I don't believe he had ever been in the South. He quickly learned to love barbeque. He also learned to appreciate the gentle ways in which business is done in the small towns where we were shooting. About the third day he was there, I even saw him smile.

～

Forever after, I would from time to time be walking down the hallway of the Columbia executive suites and hear a voice ring out, "Harry, when are you going to find us another picture to shoot in Arkansas?" It was always Seymour and always with a smile.

The Blue and the Gray engaged an all-star cast with some of the biggest stars of the era—Warren Oats, Colleen Dewhurst, Rip Torn, Geraldine Page, Lloyd Bridges, Stacy Keach, Gregory Peck, and many more.

Over the course of the months we were on location, I was the producer who would have to fly back to Los Angeles every few weeks to report directly to Seymour and management on how things were going.

If he had four or five consecutive days off, Stacy Keach would often accompany me back to L.A. There were no direct flights out of Fayetteville to Los Angeles, so my friend, Hayden McIlroy, helped to arrange a time-saving way for us to travel.

About every other Thursday, I drove to the Fayetteville

airport (with Stacy sometimes joining me) to travel west. It was always the same. As we boarded a twin-engine plane, the pilots were already in the cockpit, pre-flighting the aircraft. In the cabin area, there was always a distinguished, handsome, white-headed man in the smaller passenger jump seat and some of his employees in the rear two seats. We would always say, "Sir, one of us will ride in the jump seat. You take a normal seat, it's your plane!" He always replied graciously, "No, thanks, I'm fine, plus I may want to fly the plane for awhile myself," which—as a licensed pilot himself—he sometimes did.

After a very short flight to Oklahoma City, we would get off the small plane and be driven in a cart directly to the boarding stairs of our flight to Los Angeles. We never even went inside the terminal. Life was good.

Stacy, a good man, would always tell the stranger how much he appreciated the ride and how gracious he was to ride in the jump seat. The man would always pat us on the back and say no problem and how great it was to have us on board and shooting in North Arkansas. Once, getting onto our L.A. flight, Stacy asked, "What's that gentlemen's name again?"

"Sam." I answered.

"What did you tell me he does?"

"He has some variety stores and every Thursday he comes over here to check how his stores in this area are doing."

"Well, he's a gracious man. I wish him good luck."

⌣

I saw Stacy across the room at a Hollywood event many years

later. Momentarily, he came up to me and said, "Harry! After years, I figured out who that good man on the plane with us was. It was Walton. Sam Walton! The founder of Walmart!" We both smiled.

It was indeed Sam Walton, the founder of Walmart. I thought I had told Stacy the name of the store at the time but I guess I hadn't. Walmart had quite a few stores then but was far from the giant it is now. At that time, its stores were only in Arkansas and a few surrounding states. People outside the area barely knew the chain existed.

Stacy and I knew one thing—the company was led by a kind and generous gentleman.

Johnny Carson and the Sax Man

MY WIFE, THE INCREDIBLE LINDA BLOODWORTH THOMASON whom I love dearly, detects the American pulse better than anyone I have ever known.

It wasn't long after we got married that she met Bill and Hillary Clinton. I asked her what she thought, and she said they would both probably be president someday.

I am not going to fill this book with Clinton stories.... Just this one and the rest another time—in another book.

We invited the Clintons to come out to the studio in the mid-eighties and held an event for all the people at Columbia (Sony) Studios to meet them. We told everybody that Bill would probably run for president sometime in the nineties. Linda and I introduced the then Governor-Clinton and Hillary to the people who might someday help, should he decide to run. Bill Clinton has always been charismatic. At the time, he was a very popular governor and chairman of the National Governors Association. People were drawn to him.

We were excited when we heard Bill had been chosen by Massachusetts Governor Michael Dukakis to speak during the 1988 Democratic National Convention in Atlanta. Clinton was a great speaker and he seemed a natural to represent the younger Democratic leadership to a national audience. Again, Linda and I told everyone we knew in Hollywood to make sure to watch because we were confident he would run for president someday.

We left our Los Angeles offices early and went home so we could see his triumphant speech live. In the convention hall, thirty-five thousand were on hand when he started to speak.

Clinton made a gigantic impression with his convention speech. Gigantic! But it wasn't a gigantic *good* impression—it was a gigantic *bad* impression. First of all, a cardinal convention rule was violated. I have always had a suspicion that it was violated by someone who wanted to eliminate some competition before the next presidential election, but that's another story. The violation was that the house lights were left fully up for his speech. That encouraged conversation and commotion among delegates. There was no way the audience could focus on the speaker. Sure enough, the convention hall crowd was restless, creating a distraction for the TV audience across the nation.

The person who advised Clinton on the length of his speech was wrong for whatever reasons. Clinton was supposed to have spoken fifteen minutes. Instead, he spoke for thirty-three agonizing minutes under bright lights with lots of competing noise.

How bad was it? It was so bad that when he neared the end

and said, "and in conclusion," the crowd went wild with applause.

∽

We watched, as the rest of the night, the national press just kept repeating that Clinton had just destroyed any future presidential hopes he might have had. It was hard not to believe it. Soon, friends were calling and saying how sorry they were that he had killed his chance at the presidency.

We were despondent the rest of the night, falling deeper into a hole as Johnny Carson came on and made fun of the speech. No rest tonight.

Sometime around daybreak, Linda punched me, "Are you awake?"

"I am now."

"Listen to me. I know what he has to do to repair this."

I was a little sarcastic, "Really? That would have to be a pretty good fix!"

She told me, "He has to go on *The Tonight Show* with Carson and redeem himself. You have to get to the office as soon as you can and get in touch with Johnny."

"You say that like Johnny Carson is a friend of ours! How am I going to get in touch with Johnny?"

"Just get up and get going. You'll figure it out."

I was in the office early with not many ideas when I finally thought of someone who could help. I dialed David Horowitz—the beloved and celebrated public relations guy who handled such things for *Designing Women*. "David, it's Harry."

He replied, "I am so sorry about Clinton last night."

"Yeah, that's why I'm calling. Do you know Johnny Carson?"

"Well, I've met him many times but wouldn't say he was a good friend. Freddy DeCordova, his producer, I know well. Why?"

"Linda thinks the only way our friend can redeem himself is to get on Johnny's show."

"That's a good idea but will probably be tough. It's not like Clinton is known across the nation."

I replied with more sarcasm than intended, "Well, he's known well enough for Carson to make fun of him on his show last night."

"I hear you, let me call DeCordova and check it out. Be back to you when I have heard something."

I called the Governor's Mansion and found out that the Clintons would not return from Atlanta until later that night.

Around noon, "David Horowitz for you on line one."

"Harry, I did the best I could. He says Johnny has never had a politician on the show and he's not going to start now. I'm sorry, I pressed it hard."

"I know you did David, I know you did. Thanks for trying." I hung up despondent.

Linda called after lunch and I told her the news. "You can't give up. We can't let this happen to your friend." After we had a brief argument about the prospects for intervention, she convinced me to try again, with a little different tack this time.

I called David. "David, he won't be coming on as a politician, he will be appearing with his saxophone as Bill Clinton, the musician." David laughs but he agrees to try to get DeCordova on the line and explain that Clinton will come on and play a number with the band or whatever they want.

DeCordova was silent for a long moment, then said, "I'll go to Johnny and ask but I don't think he will agree. Harry, have you already talked to Clinton about it?"

I swallowed hard. "Yes, and he is all for it!"

"Good, let me go down the hall to Johnny. I'll be back to you."

Fifteen minutes later the phone rang. It was DeCordova. "I'm shocked but your friend is on *The Tonight Show* this Tuesday night, playing with the band. Tell Clinton to start working out his saxophone right now. It's got to be better than that speech. Doc Severinsen wants to know what song Clinton wants to play so he can get the band ready."

"Thanks so much! I will call you back on Monday with details."

DeCordova got off as David stayed on the line a little longer. David said, "I know you haven't talked to Clinton, but you'd better—in a hurry. If this falls through, you and I will be in trouble. Freddy told me they are going to announce it on tonight's show."

It was around nine o'clock when I tried the Governor's Mansion in Little Rock again. Hillary came to the phone, "Harry, Bill is not here, he's out jogging." After an awkward beat she said, "It was pretty bad, right?"

"It was sort of ugly. Whoever left the lights up should be shot."

She laughed and said, "Well he went way too long, and that was our fault."

I hesitated, and then, "I ... know this ... is crazy, but I just booked your husband on the Johnny Carson show for Tuesday night." An uneasy silence followed. My anxiety rose, "Is that okay?"

Another pause, then, "It is more than okay, it's great! I can't think of anything better at the moment. I will have him call you the minute he gets back in. I am not going to mention what it is, I'll let you do that." She laughed and we hung up.

Forty-five minutes later the phone rang, "Harry, it's Bill. Hillary said you needed to talk to me?"

"Governor, you are booked to appear on the Carson show on Tuesday night."

A moment passed, then, "You know, while I was out jogging, trying to think about what to do—that was it. That, maybe, I could go on his show and help things a little!"

"Well, you'll have your chance this Tuesday night."

"I'm grateful, I really am. Thank you."

"You're welcome, but there's something else."

"What?"

"You're playing the saxophone with Doc Severinsen and the band."

"You're kidding!"

"Nope, can you do it?"

A beat, "Do I have a choice?"

"Nope."

"Then, I'm looking forward to it!"

I told him to call me on Saturday with the name of the song he wanted to play.

Saturday morning, I got a call from the governor's office. It wasn't the Governor, it was his chief of staff. "Harry, the Governor filled us in on everything. We've just had a staff meeting and decided he should do *The Tonight Show*, but we think it is undignified for him to play the sax on the show. We need to scratch that."

I was tired and after very little sleep in days, I had to listen to this guy—one of the nicest guys in the world—but I went ballistic anyway, "What the hell are you talking about? Does the governor know this is your decision?"

"No, we just made it and were about to call him, just wanted to tell you first."

"Listen, I want to make this f**king clear—the only damn reason he is going on the show is to play the sax—being the damn governor counts for zero! If he is not going to play the sax, then Carson doesn't want to see him!"

"Okay, okay, calm down, we get it."

I felt embarrassed I had lost it and I did calm down a bit, "I'm sorry! I've already told the Governor. He knows."

"He didn't mention it but I get it. What can I do to help?"

"Make him choose his song and start practicing today."

On Monday we advised *The Tonight Show* that Clinton would play the Gershwin classic "Summertime" on the show.

On Tuesday, Clinton, Hillary and some of his staff arrived in town. Late that afternoon, we left our offices at the Burbank studio and headed for NBC. Once backstage at *The Tonight Show,* a production assistant showed us to the dressing room. Linda started going over some things Bill might say (not that he needed any help). She then gave him a huge hourglass and told him that when he goes out, he should hide it the best he can and when Carson asks the very first question, he should pull it out and—in a grand gesture—plant it on the desk. The governor thought that was funny.

Freddie DeCordova appeared and introduced himself, as we heard the show starting, the applause and the band playing. DeCordova walked us to the wings as Clinton licked the reed of his horn in preparation for stepping onto the stage. As Linda handed Bill the hourglass, DeCordova totally panicked. "No, what are you doing? Take that away from him!"

Puzzled, we grab it away from Clinton just in time to hear Carson say, "Arkansas Governor, Bill Clinton!!!"

The applause (and a little laughter) was deafening as Bill made his way onto the stage and sat. Carson, grinning, reached under his desk and pulled out an even bigger hourglass than ours, and—smiling broadly—turned it up on his desk. "How are you, governor?" The crowd laughed hysterically.

What followed was an audience and a nation (one of the highest-rated shows of the season) changing its mind and falling in love with the young governor from Arkansas. The saxophone number was a big hit. People were on their feet cheering at the end.

After the show, with the help of our dear friend, Amy

Baker from NBC, we had arranged a party at a nearby boutique hotel. We had invited some Los Angeles people we thought the Clintons should know. At the end of a wonderful night, we took everybody's picture under a banner that said, BILL CLINTON FOR PRESIDENT 1996.

We wouldn't have to wait that long.

J. Weintraub.

MAYBE YOU DIDN'T KNOW HIM. Maybe you just knew his popular movies, ranging from *Diner* to *Karate Kid* and *Ocean's Eleven*. Or maybe you saw the great documentary about him *My Way* on HBO.

I had always heard of him, but our paths had never crossed. That all changed the day before Thanksgiving 1992.

The presidential election was only a few weeks behind us. Linda and I had been fortunate enough to help with the campaign of our longtime friend, Bill Clinton, whom my brother, Danny, as mentioned earlier, had introduced me to in 1968. During the presidential campaign, I had concentrated on the convention and election night, while Linda produced the watermark film, *The Man From Hope*.

Hurrying to finish the paperwork on my desk and start the holiday, I was interrupted by my assistant, Carole, standing in the doorway, "There is someone who says he is from Camp David on the phone ... And he wants to talk to you."

"What? It must be a joke. Bill doesn't take office, until January. Who would I know at Camp David?".

"I'm just telling you what he said," Carole replied.

Reluctant but curious, I picked up the phone and spoke tentatively, "Hello."

A military-sounding voice replied, "Is this Mr. Thomason?"

"Yes, it is ..."

"Sir, this is the operator at Camp David. Someone here would like to speak to you." A click. "Mr. Weintraub, Mr. Thomason is on the line"

A cheery, booming voice speaks, "Harry?"

"Yes?"

"You don't know me but ..."

I interrupted, "No, I've never met you, but I certainly know who you are."

He chuckled and continued, "We're here for Thanksgiving and we were talking, and President Bush thought there were some things I should tell you."

Okay, I knew Jerry Weintraub was a famous movie producer and I knew he was a friend of President George H.W. Bush ... But I couldn't imagine what the heck the president of the United States would want him to tell me. Just for the record, having been on the presidential debate production team, I had met President Bush several times, and found him to be one of the kindest human beings on Earth. But I digress.

Jerry spoke, "You know, I've been a friend of George's for a long time just like you have with the kid from Arkansas that just beat him. The president wants me to tell you what's going to happen to you."

"What?"

"You and Linda are going to be accused of everything short of murder. You're going to be forced to spend a fortune in legal fees. You'll probably be dragged before grand juries. Everything you have ever recorded or written will be subpoenaed." My head was beginning to ache as he continued a litany of horrible plagues about to be visited upon us.

Finally, I spoke, "How do you know this?"

After a brief pause,"Because, I'm an old, close friend of George's and everything I described happened to me just because of that. George wanted me to warn you about what will probably happen to you."

I heard President Bush in the background say, "Don't forget to tell him about the congressional hearings."

Not really knowing how to respond, I finally said, "Jerry, I appreciate this call and I understand."

A quick retort, "No, you don't understand ... But you will."

Two years into President Clinton's first term, I was beginning to understand. I didn't help myself by meddling in things I shouldn't have. But meddle I did, and that started the circus.

I was commanded to appear before a grand jury where the prosecutor spent most of his time talking about what a sorry place Hollywood was. In fact, his aspersions aggravated me so that we ended in a verbal brawl—and almost in an old-fashioned fistfight. The jury had to be recessed. We finally apologized to each other, and he turned out to be an okay guy.

Every piece of paper Linda and I ever had was confiscated. Investigators even took our computers—well maybe they didn't get all of them. One day, I was driving down the street in Los Angeles when my cell phone rang. It was some congressional aide saying she had just gotten word that I was burning and destroying papers even as we spoke.

"Ma'am, I'm driving down Ventura Boulevard to buy dog food, and you are crazy as a loon!" I probably did not endear myself to a lot of people whose paths I crossed at that time.

Oh, and remember Jerry said I would be—as he had been—accused of everything short of murder? Well, I got the murder rap. Bill Safire of the *New York Times* said he thought I was guilty of murder. Safire is no longer with us. No, though the thought crossed my mind at the time, I did not kill him.

It never occurred to me that any of Jerry's phone call was "sour grapes," nor was it a threat by the losing candidate. Everything Jerry told me was going to happen to me did—just as it had happened to him. He and President Bush just wanted to warn me.

I wanted to thank them for preparing me for the onslaught. So, almost two years later, I put in a phone call to Warner Bros. Studio and asked if they could connect me to Jerry Weintraub. A phone rang, a voice answered and she identified herself. It was someone who had worked for us when we were on the lot—a piece of luck! "Norma, how are you?" We had a good conversation, catching up on things, and then I asked if I could speak to Jerry.

I asked her not to tell him who was calling, just get him on the phone.

"Harry, he hates that, he will want to know who is calling!"

"Just try it!"

Soon Jerry picked up, growling into the phone, "Hello. Who *is* this?"

After two years, I waited one more beat before saying, "Jerry, I understand."

Another beat, then a large laugh, "Harry, I've been wondering when I would hear from you!" We had a great conversation and I told him how much I appreciated his heads-up on that Thanksgiving eve in 1992.

Both President Bush and Jerry left us way too soon.

〜

Tbilisi in the Rear-View Mirror

LINDA AND I WERE IN WASHINGTON FOR A FEW DAYS IN 1993 on one of our visits with our old friend who was now the president. There I talked to another friend, Under Secretary of State Strobe Talbot who happened to be married to Brooke Shearer, private investigator, U.S. Interior Department, Hillary Clinton aide and good friend. Talbot asked if we wanted to go to an event with him that night. Linda was committed to another function, but I said I would go.

Off I went to a dinner for Eduard Shevardnadze, the head of state of the country of Georgia. Georgia had just broken away from the old, collapsing Soviet Union. The relationship was rocky with Russia still trying to exert some control over Georgia. Plus, Abkhazia—a part of Georgia—had broken away from Georgia and there was vicious fighting going on throughout the state.

It was a very pleasant, low-key event and the evening ended with everyone singing happy birthday to Shevardnadze's wife, Nanuli.

Several weeks later, back in our office in Los Angeles, my new secretary said, "Someone named Strobe Talbot is on the phone." Strobe told me that the U.S. would like to get some medical aid to Georgian children's hospitals which were suffering from insufficient beds and medicines, a problem exacerbated by an influx of casualties.

The State Department wanted to keep everything as low profile as they could since Georgia was still on shaky terms with the Russians. The U.S. didn't want to cause acting Head of State Shevardnadze any discomfort. Talbot said Dr. Trish Blair, founder and president of A Call To Serve (ACTS), the first humanitarian and development organization to work in Georgia after the collapse of the Soviet Union, was leading the effort. Dr. Blair had been in Georgia with a medical team doing what she could to help the desperate situation. She was also the sister of a person I knew well: Jim Blair, a high powered, nationally known attorney in Arkansas and a friend of Bill Clinton. Jim was also good friends with one of my best friends, Hayden McIlroy.

Hayden's great-great-grandfather donated the land that the University of Arkansas is built on. Hayden is known among us as The Better Angel. Always ready to help, he is a tough businessman who has participated in some of the most forward-thinking financial innovations of our time. He is brilliant, a great storyteller and a bold adventurer. Hayden's wife, Mary Jo, is smart and funny. A character played by Annie Potts on Linda's classic television series *Designing Women*, is named after her.

I asked Strobe what I could do and he said, "There's a

medical emergency in the Republic of Georgia. I need you to get sixteen-thousand pounds of medical supplies to the capital—Tbilisi—ASAP!"

If one needed to do something important, I knew of no better guy to help out than Hayden McIlroy. With Hayden's help, a plan was developed. The medical supplies were being assembled in Miami where, with the help of aviation expert Darnel Martins, we had a waiting plane—lent by a benevolent aviation company. A Boeing 727. It wasn't the ideal plane, it was a short-range aircraft, meaning we would have to make frequent stops on our way to this far-eastern European country.

∿

On the day before we were to leave, I ran into a friend of mine, Huell Howser, in a restaurant. Originally from Nashville, Huell had a tremendously popular TV show, *California Gold,* on all thirteen PBS stations in California. I told him what was going on and he immediately asked if he could come, along with his well-known and popular cameraman and editor, Luis Fuerte, to do a story. Glad to have them, I told Huell to be at the Van Nuys airport at eight the next morning.

Our first clue that it was going to be a difficult trip came as we taxied toward the runway in our small jet at Van Nuys, California. A fuel truck clipped our wing tip, shattering a navigation light. After a three-hour inspection and repair job, we were finally underway. We would pick up Hayden in Dallas before flying on to Miami, where the 727 awaited.

We reached Miami after dark. After deplaning and stretching

our legs, we started boarding the 727, where we were welcomed by Dr. Blair and her staff. They had been in the U.S. desperately raising money to alleviate the medical crisis in Georgia. Just as I was getting on the plane, I was called back down the stairway, someone wanted to talk to me. A person in a dark suit introduced himself and told me I was having a meeting with Head of State, Shevardnadze—it was news to me. He handed me a sealed manila envelope and asked me to give it to Shevardnadze. Then he turned and vanished into the darkness.

The plane was full of supplies and only had nine passenger seats. I saw three sleeping bags on the floor. We had five pilots who had volunteered to fly in shifts, so we never stopped for any time longer than to refuel. While we were still introducing ourselves to each other, we were rolling down Miami airport runway 27 Left, on a goodwill mission—toward more adventure than we had bargained for.

In the darkness, we headed up the East Coast, eventually passing the breathtaking nighttime skyline of New York City toward our first stop, Reykjavik, Iceland, to refuel. The fuel trucks were waiting and we were quickly off toward our next stop, Dublin, Ireland. It was daybreak when we left Ireland and proceeded to Istanbul, Turkey, to refuel one last time. We actually had a chance to get off the plane in Istanbul because we had to hold for clearance into Georgian airspace—Georgia was a new county, but its airspace was still controlled by Russia. The tension registered very high on the weird scale. I think everyone on our team made eye contact with each other, conducting semi-conscious gut-checks.

∼

We landed at a dark airport in Tbilisi at 1:45 a.m. on a runway with no lights. Power was scarce in Georgia, leaving our pilots no choice. We were worn out and just wanted to get to the hotel and get some sleep. A stunning sight awaited us when the door opened and we started down the stairs!

Georgian dignitaries, military people, and their wives were everywhere. Retired Generals from WWII, in full dress uniform, their chests decorated with so many medals you couldn't count them. Over forty people. They had planned an elaborate dinner for us. Hayden and I said, "Don't bother, it's late and it's our fault so just go home." They would have none of it. They had been expecting us since seven o'clock. They had planned a banquet and we were going to have a banquet. There was unbelievably great food, music—and most of all—vodka!

Vodka was everywhere. Beside each place setting was a water pitcher, but instead of water, it was filled with vodka. We were told it would be rude not to drink it—a problem for me, since I am a non-drinker. But my good friend Huell was sitting beside me and I explained how he was going to have to drink my pitcher also! Being from Nashville and a good guy, he said he would attempt to do what he could. He did well. He would pour a glass full from his pitcher and then drink it and then I would pour a glass from mine, slide it to him and he would drink it. The drinking, conversation and goodwill went on until after 4 a.m. when they herded us back into cars and took us to our hotel. My friend Huell Howser was not feeling well.

I made it to my hotel room around 4:30 a.m. and before I fell into bed, I stepped outside the room onto a small window balcony. The sun would not make an appearance for another hour. I could hear automatic gunfire in the distance. A dog's bark echoed through the night. The night sounds reminded me there was still war going on in Georgia. I was a long way from Hampton, my carefree youth, and my brothers, Danny and Ted the dog.

Three hours later, we are all up and in a hospital filled with frightened, sick, scared, burned, and wounded children who needed angels like Dr. Blair and her team. It was so depressing to see the conditions this hospital was operating under. Electrical power was intermittent and waiting rooms were overflowing with injured and burned children. Huell was planning on shooting the sort of uplifting episode that his show was famous for, but this was a tough one to feel uplifted about, except that Dr. Trish and her valiant team were doing all they could.

At noon, I broke off and was transported to the State Office in downtown Tbilisi for a meeting. I was escorted into Eduard Shevardnadze's office and through an interpreter we were introduced. I handed him the strange manila envelope I had been carrying since I left Miami. An aide took it and left the room. Shevardnadze said something and the interpreter said. "He says you look familiar."

I replied, "Yes, we met in Washington. I was with my friend Strobe Talbot and we sang happy birthday to your wife."

His eyes sparkled and he laughed and said, "Yes, a very good night!" We talked through the interpreter for a few minutes about where we each grew up and that sort of thing. He told me how much he cared for President Clinton. A pleasant conversation ensued about a wide range of topics including even the entertainment business. He loved Gregory Peck, who I also loved and had worked with. I then told him I had taken enough of his time and would excuse myself.

He frowned and spoke, "And you just got here after midnight?"

"Yes sir."

He said, "You have to be tired, why don't you come to my dacha (country house) with Nanuli and me and have a restful weekend?"

"I would love to sir, but it is my wife's birthday this weekend and I want to be back with her."

He laughed and said, "I understand. Maybe, I should sing happy birthday to her since you sang to my wife." Alas, my cell phone was drained when I needed it most. We shook hands, and I went back out onto the streets of Tbilisi. Hayden and I walked the old, elegant city for a while.

When we got back to the hotel, I ran into Huell, who was discouraged about the state of affairs he and his cinematographer had found on the streets. Huell expressed his intuition that a bleak future awaited the people of Georgia.

The people of Tbilisi sure knew how to celebrate. Hayden informed me that Dr. Trish just told him the Georgians wanted to throw one more party for us. When we arrived at our hotel, the hospitable Georgians were waiting for us with another gathering and dinner. As Luis, the cameraman said, "Even as tired as we were, how could we refuse?"

We learned that the Georgians had made a considerable effort to find food for our dinner—they wanted to show us kindness and friendship even though they had so little to share. Everyone again attempted to drink a portion of gallons of vodka in pitchers, except me. I kept going to the bathroom and pouring my drink out because Huell had informed me that he "... would be off double drinking duty tonight." There was singing, dancing and celebration. Air in the room grew hazy and reeked of the cigarettes everyone seemed to be smoking. We were anxious to leave, and after some time, Dr. Blair drove us through the darkness to the airport.

We all hugged Dr Blair and her staff goodbye and wished them luck. The crew of the 727 fired up the aircraft and the pilots taxied the aircraft into position at the end of the runway. They asked for permission to take off and we waited—and waited. Then, we taxied back toward the tower and one of the pilots came back and whispered to Hayden and me, "For some damn reason they are refusing to give us permission to leave. The tower and this airspace are still under Russian control."

We were tired but this is certainly got our attention.

Soon, Hayden and I were in the control tower with Dr. Blair, the pilots, one Russian Army private, two heavy-set Russian women, and the control tower operators. One of the women, explained it in simple terms, "In order for you to take off, you have to pay us, the Russian government, ten thousand in American dollars as a landing fee."

The pilots, who flew internationally on a regular basis, were fuming saying no such rule existed. The Russian Army private testily assured them it was a standard practice. Dr. Trish phoned the Georgian health minister, who came to the tower. The minister was mad, shouting "This is not something the Russians can do."

The Russians ignored him.

Exasperated, we called the U.S. Embassy, where a man could only say he would call us back. We wondered when that might happen.

Thirty-five minutes later, he called to say the U.S. Embassy had to be extraordinarily careful not to expose their involvement in our predicament. He said he would start calling some people he needed to talk to in the U.S. and would call us back shortly. I pleaded with the Russian women that we came here on a mercy mission and they should not charge us. They said, "Rules are rules," and walked away.

We waited and waited for the State Department to call us back. Finally, they called and asked to speak to one of our pilots. We handed the phone over. Our pilot listened intently, just saying, "Uh huh" every so often, his brow frequently furrowed

After our pilot hung up, he conferred with the other pilots—I believe all were former military pilots. When they finished, he motioned for Hayden and me to join him outside. Once the door was closed, he said, "Okay, the person I was just talking to says it puts everybody in an awkward position if the State Department has to be visible in this." Hayden and I groan as he continued,

"But, he put someone else on the line and they revealed that, though Russia still controls the airspace, they have no aircraft in this country." I thought I knew where this was going, and a shiver ran through me.

The pilot continued. Having talked to his guys, he agreed that if we could get in the air, we would have enough time—with about fifteen minutes to spare—to reach Turkish airspace before the Russians could scramble aircraft and catch up with us. Hayden and I had him go over it in more detail. We were of the same opinion. It was a good option.

We then put the plan to Dr. Blair. As she was staying in Georgia, our concern was that our unauthorized escape might hurt her organization's ability to continue their work.

We put the plan in action. I told the two Russian women that the State Department was on their way with the ten thousand dollars in cash, due to arrive within thirty minutes. Excited, they shook our hands almost painfully. The Russian Army private came over and patted us on the back. After we all "celebrated" for a moment, we inquired—since we were running so late—if we could proceed to restart the engines and taxi to the runway, so we could go the minute they deliver the money? I held my breath as they discussed it among themselves. After a moment, they said yes. Back in the plane, we informed Huell and Luis. They did not hesitate. Huell said, "Let's go home! I've got a headache."

We taxied into position and waited. After about three minutes, we had one of the pilots radio the tower to tell them we had just heard from the state department and the money should be there in five minutes or so. One of the women replied, "Yes, we see a car coming toward us now." We didn't know what or who was in the car, but it seemed to be the trigger. The pilot said, "I say let's go, *now!*"

We all responded together, "Let's go!"

The throttles were jammed forward and the old 727 roared to life. In a few seconds, we started moving down the runway. We heard the three Russians screaming and cursing into the radio for us to stop! As we lifted off, we could see them in the tower gesturing at us! I didn't realize that extending the middle finger was a sign of unhappiness *in many countries.*

Once airborne, every person on board was looking out of the windows for hostile aircraft. The minutes counted down, the tension grew, but all we saw outside was darkness. And darkness never looked so good.

After what seemed an eternity, someone said, "Three minutes to safety." They were the longest one hundred and eighty seconds of my life. The end of those three minutes was punctuated by a loud cheer—we could see lights on the coast of Turkey below us. The only way to describe it is *exhilarating.*

We cheered one more time on that long trip home, it was when we saw the New York skyline off to our right. Finally, we felt safely *home* and knew that Tbilisi was in the rear-view mirror.

The Snake Oil Salesman

ONE DAY IN THE MID 1990s, I WAS IN LAS VEGAS for the wedding of my friend Amy Baker, a former NBC executive. The ceremony was held in an elegant home, beautifully decorated, with an orchestra playing poolside. I arrived late and hurried to my assigned table where five other guests were already seated. As I eased into my chair, I nodded hello to the other tablemates including an elderly man, round-faced, with a jowly chin, sitting right beside me. As I looked at him, he glanced back with something between a smile and scowl. I was about to speak when he beat me to it, "Son, do you know who I am?"

~

I saw his name on the place card and suddenly it's a hot morning in the summer of 1949. I'm nine years old as I walk into my father's grocery store in South Arkansas. Dad is talking to a couple of guys as I ease in beside him and he puts an arm around my shoulder. Tom, a big, burley, jowly guy in a Panama hat, preaches the benefits of a product he is selling. He stops and tells the other guy to take over. Obviously, Tom is training his associate to sell the product. My dad listens as the guy drones on for a few minutes. Then, Dad interrupts, "What is the product called, again?"

"Hadacol, the greatest non-prescription medicine ever put on store shelves. You won't be able to keep it in stock. It's good for everything that ails you and your customers are going to keep coming back." I lose interest and move to Ted, the bulldog/security guard for my brother, Danny, and me. I got the feeling Ted did not like these guys who were bellowing the benefits of this bottle in a carton labeled Hadacol.

The big guy was very persuasive and my dad bought cartons of the stuff, much to the chagrin of my mom, who thought our little store would never be able to sell it.

After the selling was over the big guy walked over to me: "Son, there is gonna be a show at the high school auditorium tonight and you have to have a Hadacol box top to get in. Here's four, you bring your brother and your mom and dad. You're gonna have fun." And with that he grabbed his understudy and walked out of the store.

Well, we went to the Hadacol show that night. I had never seen anything like it. Here we were in a small town in South Arkansas and it was like we were at a Broadway revue. There was a variety of music acts. The barker claimed the talent was well-known to radio audiences nationally. Many years later, I found out that Hank Williams did the Hadacol show and so did noted performers like George Burns and Gracie Allen, names that would be big for years to come. I don't think they were in the Hampton, Arkansas, edition but they could have been. Dog acts, dance numbers, you name it and they had it! Oh, and they had a magician. He was great! He made flowers appear from nowhere and he made other things disappear. He even pointed to me in the audience and invited me to the stage! My head was swimming. As I mounted the steps, I was so excited I could barely breathe.

The big man had a large, jeweled box with a lid on it. He opened it. The inside was totally filled with two side-by-side giant white dice with black dots. He let me look at it, examine the dice and then he showed the audience the box and dice with a large flourish. The music started (yes, there was even a band accompanying him). He whipped his magic cape across the box. Then he asked me to open the box. I reached up and pulled the lid slowly open ... The dice were no longer there, and the crowd cheered wildly. I was mesmerized. But wait, I saw something odd, a speck of white, on the edge of the box. I realized what had happened. Excited, I knew how he did it. This was great! The dice were hollow, and when he swept his cape across the box, he also turned it over and opened the underside, which showed only the black-painted inside of the dice. I was exhilarated and inspired to share my discovery with the audience! I reached for one of the dice, to flip it over. My hand arrived there just as he pulled the box away. I stepped forward to reach it again. This time, I looked up at the magician to see how proud he was of me for learning the trick.

He was not. His eyes were telling me with all the energy he could silently muster not to expose him. The audience was still applauding and the band still playing when I heard him speak in something close to a ventriloquist voice, "Kid, please don't do it."

I thought for a minute. After reflecting for an instant on how bad it would be if he killed me on stage in front of my mother, I pulled my hand back and made an amazed face to celebrate the disappearance of the dice. As the applause died down, I was escorted off stage. Taking one fleeting look back at the magician, I saw him mouth "thanks" to me.

When we got home from that exhilarating night, I told my mom what happened, and she assured me I did the right thing.

Our store sold every bottle of Hadacol it had the next day. Dad had to order more cartons from somewhere in Louisiana. It became the rage of most of the nation. There was even a song that was near the top of both country and popular lists by various artists called the *Hadacol Boogie*. Every little old lady in my hometown bought several bottles of the stuff every week. Finally my mom just had to try it. She opened a bottle, took a spoonful, and immediately spit it out! "My gosh, it's almost pure alcohol! Everyone in town must be drunk!" No, it wasn't pure alcohol, but it certainly had a lot in it. Before long, national regulators were cracking down on it. Soon it faded away—probably when the alcohol content was forcibly lowered.

∽

Suddenly, I was back at the table in Las Vegas, looking at the guy from West Virginia who had the slightly-off Southern accent and had just asked if I knew who he was. I did know him. I knew him as a music manager who had not allowed one of the world's top singers to ever reach the heights he could have, never let his client become the movie star in meaningful movies that he wanted to be, and rarely let his client go overseas as much as he wanted. This guy sitting next to me at the table was afraid to let his client travel alone because someone might tell the truth about how his manager was scamming him. He probably also thought he might be arrested if he went back to where he was really from— not West Virginia but Europe (Holland). People have always speculated on how he got into this country and what he was afraid of—tales ranging from embezzlement to murder.

As I unfolded the napkin and placed it in my lap, I eyed Colonel Tom Parker, the guy who pretty much ruined Elvis Presley's life. "Yes sir, I know you. You're the Hadacol man."

A pause. A look. "You *do* know me." A pleasant dinner followed.

Chuck Berry

I was producing Bill Clinton's 1992 Inaugural and I wanted Chuck Berry to perform at an event. I talked to his manager and he said he wasn't sure but that he would talk to Chuck and get back to me. A day later, an excited aide barged into my meeting, Chuck Berry was on the phone, "and wants to discuss something with you."

I went to my office and picked up the phone. "Hello."

Chuck spoke, "Harry, I know it's for the president. I like this guy, but I don't perform for free."

"I know you don't, Chuck. I'm planning to get you some money."

We agreed upon a very fair price and then he added one last requirement. "Now, the other thing is, I have to be paid in cash."

"Chuck, that may be hard, with all the election laws and stuff. I can get you a cashier's check."

A beat. "Naw, it's the government. I have to be paid in cash or I can't do it."

~

I was waiting in the wings with the full amount in hundred-dollar bills as he made his entrance onto the stage. "Not just picking on you, Son, I always get cash. Too many boys, including the government, have tried to screw me before."

"I get it Chuck, I get it."

I handed him the cash, which he quickly stashed in his old guitar case. "Watch it till I get back." He smiled and strode on stage, where he enthralled the screaming audience for half an hour. The crowd was screaming, clapping and on their feet. As I watched him mesmerize the crowd, I thought it would have been worth twice this much to see a performance like this. Little did I know that a chance to see another Chuck Berry performance would come a few years later.

~

1997. The Summit of Eight—a gathering of the most powerful leaders in the world was to take place in Denver, and the U.S. State Department asked me to produce the entertainment for the event. As I started putting it together, I thought of Chuck and called his manager. Chuck called me back for a few details and I told him we have very little money. He replied, "Okay, I'll do it for you for $10,000, but remember—all cash. I don't trust any of these guys."

In Denver, I explained the rules and the price to the State Department aides. They couldn't believe he wouldn't take a U.S. Treasury check. I assured them he would not and that they should get the cash together. Muttering, they left in a slight huff.

Showtime! We delivered major acts and 5,000 people in a rodeo arena. It was going well.

I was seated at the director's console in the rear of the arena. Suddenly, an ashen faced State Department guy appeared, tugging my arm. I turned to face him, "What's wrong?"

"Harry, it's Chuck. He wants to see you. He says he is not going on!"

I scrambled backstage to find Chuck in conversation with several State Department aides. "Chuck, what's the problem?"

A State Department guy interrupts, "I'll tell you what's wrong, he says he's not going out without cash and I have right here a U.S. Treasury Department certified check!" Chuck looks at me and raises an eyebrow.

After a beat, I addressed the State Department detail, "Listen, I told you well ahead of time that he only accepts cash. What was so hard to understand about that?"

"Yeah, but we thought he would take a Treasury check."

"Well, he won't. How much do you have in the petty cash fund?"

Another aide speaks, "I think we have about $2,700."

"Okay, go get it." I ask Chuck to move away with me. "Listen Chuck, I'm sorry. If I get you the $2,700 and promise to have the rest to you by the time the show is over, will you go on? I will even give you my wallet with cards, driver's license, and everything in it to hold until you are paid." I handed him the wallet.

Chuck's hesitation lasted long enough to make my heart thump and finally he spoke. "Yeah, I'll do it." He took the wallet.

I muttered my thanks and went back to a worried gaggle of State Department aides. "All right guys, here is what you have to do to save the bacon. Leave here this instant, take your credit cards and go to every ATM machine in Denver until you can gather $7,300 dollars. Do it quickly!"

Nobody even spoke. They just dashed out. The Denver police were assisting us in every way and had at least six patrol cars outside our production offices. Soon I could hear, through the cacophony of music and applause inside the arena, the sound of multiple sirens leaving the area. It did make me smile to think about a lot of panicked young government guys in police cars racing to ATMs.

I walked back over to Chuck, "The money will be here when you come offstage."

He nodded, "Thanks, and I don't need your wallet, buddy." He tossed it to me, smiled, and walked toward the wing of the stage.

If speed is the mark of an efficient government, the State Department guys were very efficient. Within twenty-five minutes, one of them was handing me a leather briefcase filled with $7,300 in twenty-dollar bills. He spoke breathlessly, "Here it is, tell Mr. Berry to keep the briefcase with our compliments." Chuck was performing as I walked to the wing and looked out at him. He glanced my way and I waggled the briefcase. For just a moment, he smiled and then rolled right into *Johnny B. Goode*.

After the show, I shook his hand, thanked him, and walked through the semi-darkness to the backstage of the arena to help wrap. I was rolling up cable when someone tapped me on the shoulder, "Harry, I want to thank you for fulfilling a lifelong dream."

I kept rolling the cable but muttered, "Good."

"Yes, he is the rock and roller that I have always admired and never thought I would get a chance to meet." By now, I had turned around to see a guy in a Western shirt and cowboy boots. That's how I found out who was the favorite rock and roller of Prime Minister Tony Blair of England.

We'll all miss you, Chuck.

Reading Group Extras

Author Biography

HARRY THOMASON, A NATIVE OF HAMPTON, ARKANSAS, attended Southern Arkansas University on an athletic scholarship and pursued graduate studies in education at the University of Arkansas.

After college, Thomason taught art and history and was a football coach in secondary schools for six years before pursuing filmmaking as a career. He continues to lecture on politics periodically at the University of Southern California.

Mr. Thomason is married to the famed writer Linda Bloodworth Thomason, with whom he has developed the successful television series, *Designing Women* (featuring Dixie Carter, Delta Burke, Annie Potts, and Jean Smart) , *Evening Shade* (with Burt Reynolds Marilu Henner, and Charles Durning), *Hearts A'fire* (with John Ritter and Markie Post) and *Twelve Miles of Bad Road* (featuring Lily Tomlin and Ron White).

Thomason produced *The Bridegroom* documentary, created and directed by his wife Linda Bloodworth Thomason. *The*

Bridegroom won numerous awards including Best Narrative Film from the prestigious Tribeca Film Festival. He also directed the critically-acclaimed feature documentary, *The Hunting of the President*, selected for The Sundance Film Festival and the South by Southwest Festival and nominated for the Writer's Guild Best Documentary.

He directed *The Last Ride*, a feature film about the waning days of Hank Williams, and produced many award winning television movies including *A Shining Season, To Find My Son*, and the popular mini-series *The Blue and The Gray*.

For his wife, Linda, who created it, Thomason produced the film, *The Man from Hope*, which launched William Jefferson Clinton's first campaign for president. He followed that by producing the 1992 Democratic National Convention and was strategic director of the 1996 Democratic National Convention. Thomason and Linda were Co-Chairpersons of the 1993 Presidential Inauguration—the first presidential inauguration in the history of the United States to make a profit. That profit was used to help fund the 1997 inauguration, which Thomason also directed.

He produced and directed *Saturday Night at the Summit*, a live broadcast from the Summit of the Eight gathering of top world leaders in Denver Colorado.

Harry Thomason has been nominated for or won numerous film and TV awards, including the Emmy (*Designing Women, Evening Shade*), the Directors Guild Award (*Designing Women*), the Christopher Award (*A Shining Season*) and The People's Choice

Award (*The Blue and The Gray*). In 1996, he was named the Entertainment Publicists' Guild's Man of the Year.

Author Statement

How it Began

It started harmlessly enough. A legendary rock and roller died. I knew him and had a story to tell (it's in the book). I scribbled a memory on paper and then decided to post it online. Lots of response. Many wrote with variations of, "Hey, that was a good story! Why don't you write some of your other memories down in a book?" Lots of those were my ex-students and athletes who remembered me boring them in class with tales of growing up in Southern Arkansas.

I appreciate writers. My wife, Linda Bloodworth Thomason (Lucy to me), is one of the absolute best. So, I realize how much discipline it takes. She has it. I don't. After years of writing over three hundred and fifty scripts for television, she said sweetly, "Surely you can write one ... little, tiny book."

I countered, "But they're mostly just stories of me growing up in a small town."

Lucy replied, "Exactly. And no one else has them. Write

them down."

My daughter, Stacy, my brother Danny, and my thirty-eight cousins agreed, "Yeah do it. Write 'em down. Then we won't have to listen to you tell them at family reunions."

I was fortunate to have been born into a huge multi-generational family (both Thomasons and Means) where everyone loves and looks after everyone else. My thirteen aunts and uncles and their spouses were all smart and enterprising, with big hearts and open minds. And the result is their children who became doctors, scientists, lawmen, teachers, coaches, airline pilots, and you name it. All are extremely close, having been raised by all of our parents. I am undoubtedly the only slacker in the bunch. Needless to say, if I were in a foreign prison (it could easily have happened—it's in the book) and allowed only one phone call (and my wife failed to answer because she thinks call waiting is rude to the person you're already speaking with), anyone of my cousins would be my first call. Because I know, in a very short period, I would hear gunfire, and helicopters buzzing overhead.

Anyway, it's because of all these people's insistence that I have finally put pen to paper.

What followed were the memories and musings of an unusually lucky Southern boy, who was blessed to take an unusually lucky journey that's hopefully not over yet. Most of my stories about Washington and Hollywood won't be found here. I'm saving my adventures in politics and entertainment for a future edition. Or maybe just to bore my grandchildren with. We'll see how this one goes.

I believe everyone of us has a story to tell. When you have finished reading mine, you may just have an epiphany. "Hey, if this guy, who's not even a writer, can write a book—I bet I can too!"

I bet you can, too.

Questions & Answers with the Author

WHY DID YOU WRITE THIS BOOK?

I started out as a high school teacher and coach. I loved what I was doing and it was a joy to deal with students. During those six years, I noticed that the students loved it when I told them stories of my childhood and my friends' childhoods. My childhood was different than theirs and they enjoyed the comparisons. So, I thought that writing this book about growing up when I did would both preserve an era before the strangling electronic era we live in now that younger people might like to read and that mature people might like as a marker of where we were and where we are now socially.

I think it will be fun for people to look, not at the large history of our nation but at the small history of individuals grown up and getting through life of all generations. A chance to compare a time when children were not as closely monitored as they are now; they were raised by the community they lived in, before helicopter parents came on the scene.

WHAT MAKES YOUR STORY SO SPECIAL?

Every story—anybody's story—is a way to communicate that all areas of the country have different things to say. In the widely varying areas of this country, I think it would help us to know what life is like elsewhere. We are going to have to get to know each other.

I was from a family that was not afraid to express strong political opinions, but we knew how to stay friendly with people who took the other side of an issue. People understood that it was okay to strongly disagree on politics and still have close friendships.

WHAT IS THE ONE TAKEAWAY YOU WOULD WANT PEOPLE TO HAVE FROM READING YOUR BOOK?

Tell your tales. If nothing else, your friends and relatives want to hear them. Hearing your life stories may affect how friends and relatives feel about their lives and prospects—or memories.

WHAT WILL READERS LOVE ABOUT THIS BOOK?

I hope they see it as a reflection of themselves. I hope it makes them think of important memories that make them feel good and remember friends and relatives they love. I hope it evokes a better time and will help us strive for even better times and closer ties in the future.

DO YOU HAVE OTHER BOOKS IN YOU?

If people happen to be interested in this one, yes I would like to do another book. There are so many stories of my childhood that I didn't tell in this one. And I barely touched on tales of the entertainment and political fields. Look, my stories just demonstrate that we all have tales to tell.

WHAT WAS YOUR FAVORITE STORY IN THE BOOK?

I think I like the Paddy story best. It was a story that not only involved my brother Danny and our dog Ted, it involved our wonderful mother. She encouraged us and helped to make the story happen.

IF YOU HAD TO CHOOSE ONE LESSON YOU WERE TRYING TO TEACH US WITH THIS STORY, WHAT WOULD IT BE?

Unity. This is not the first time this country had been through a period of sectional differences. But when you think about it, we have many more beliefs in common than we have core beliefs that separate us. Even the late sixties and early seventies had probably more sharp edges than we do now, and we got over those. I think it will help bind us together if we just know each other's stories.

YOU ONLY LIGHTLY BRUSH POLITICS IN THIS BOOK. IF YOU WRITE ANOTHER ONE WILL YOU DEAL WITH POLITICS?

Yes, because Linda and I accidentally got way more involved in politics than we meant to! This may be surprising but my foray into politics was mostly good, not bad. Now, no doubt that most of the horrible things that Jerry Weintraub told me would happen to us did happen. Those difficulties hurt us financially because we felt we had to defend every single one, even the most minute attack on us. Eventually, we just learned to forget some of the minor attacks. But on the positive side, we got to meet a lot of people—and I don't mean just from one party. We made friends with lots of good people who were on the other side of the aisle. Washington had not turned so bitter when we were there for long periods of time. Now, there seems to be a pronounced bitterness between parties. Even so, I bet if you were there every day, you would still see signs of hope between the factions. I have so many Washington and White House stories that they alone would fill a book.

DO YOU PLAN TO SHARE MORE HOLLYWOOD STORIES IN A FUTURE BOOK?

The entertainment stories, involving people we have worked with in Hollywood, would also fill a book. I would like a chance to express why Linda and I think people that make up Hollywood film crews are the hardest working people in the nation and why they may be a better representation of the nation than any other working group.

HOW WOULD YOU BRIEFLY DESCRIBE THE BOOK TO A FRIEND?

Probably much simpler than what people think. For me, the book is a way to save the stories of my life for my beloved daughter, Stacy, and my grandchildren—Madison, Chase and Sophie.

⟶

Acknowledgements

Stacy, thank you for being the most glorious and loving daughter any man could ever hope for—and for the gift of Madison, Chase, Sophie and Mark. So proud to be your dad!

Danny, no words can express what you mean to me brother. Just keep on being there and I will too. So will Ted.

I want to express my deepest gratitude to my parents, my eighteen aunts and uncles, thirty eight first cousins and all the other wonderful family and friends who have, at some point over the years, supported, informed and inspired me from boyhood through adulthood. Hopefully, some of my best stories, involving politics and entertainment are still to come. And there are many of you out there who helped to make them memorable. But, until then, heartfelt thanks!

HAL HOLBROOK
Los Angeles, California
May, 2019

Dear Harry,

These are some of the sweetest memories I have ever read, your life as a boy in Arkansas. Reading your book made me think so strongly of the days I spent on a farm in Connecticut when I was a boy, chicken shit squeezed in between my toes. I never wore shoes all summer.

I lived at night in the attic on a bed there. If there were rats, I never knew it. It was the happiest time of my whole life. Looking back now, I think of it with a pleasure that can never be rivaled. Reading your stories, I don't know why these memories are so powerful and bring back such happy times, except they do. I made a tree house in a huge maple and I lived up there, slept at night in a contraption I built so I wouldn't fall off. It was my private domain. Nothing could ever harm me there. These are memories that you touched in writing about your youth.

I really enjoyed your stories so much, Harry, especially since I had no idea about your real upbringing in rural Arkansas. You were in the heart of it there. I should have known from the sound of your voice.

Thank you for writing this book so that I could feel I understood some of your life as a boy and what you loved about it. My treehouse is still there. I wonder if yours is.

Love,

Hal

If you have enjoyed this book, point your browser to:

www.parkhurstbrothers.com